What people are saying

"Highly recommended! Great book for both the novice reader and the well read individual. It's a common sense book on how to create balance in life. The entire book reflects Ms. Facun's sincere devotion and passion to reach out and help people."

Marissa B. Magno, Executive VP,
5 Star Alliance Inc., CA

"Outstanding! Very relevant to the needs of people today. The content of the book will be helpful to anyone. Down to earth ideas and information everyone can use."

Gloria Bernales Madarang,
teacher and writer, Singapore

"Leah is an inspirational example of success. I loved her message about being Happy, Healthy and Wealthy by following your joy and what makes you glow happiness. I appreciate how Leah encourages us to make a stance in our principles in order to achieve our dreams. Thank you Leah!"

Dr. M. Valdez, World of Health, CA

Yes! The Secrets Work! is a must read! It will give you a greater insight to life. I found a piece of me in this book and the message has elements that apply to all our lives... to help identify our personal GLOW! It's an easy read but probes self-reflection."

N. Franklin, Entrepreneur, CA

"I'm grateful to Leah for sharing her knowledge, years of experiences, and generous heart to create a book that will be helpful and practical to everyone at all walks of life. Bringing love to people's lives comes through in this book."

Amber Updike, mother, Alaska educational
experience provider, AK

"Your book served as an inspiration to me in my difficult times. To learn that you have gone through trials and have emerged victorious, without an ounce of bitterness, motivated me. Thank you for sharing your secrets. They are nuggets of wisdom that we can apply in our everyday life. I highly recommend it to others."
Ana Briones Mesina, nurse and minister, NY

"Very inspiring and encouraging! It's a book that you want to keep on reading because it is so interesting. For one thing, it holds life's truths. It should be very helpful to its readers."
Aurora P. Garcia, teacher, CA

We consider this book as a treasured gem which absolutely has enriched our lives. An absolute winning strategy which will ready-pack anyone from all walks of life. Thank you very much "Ms Leah" for your wonderful imprinted gift to mankind.
H & M Moreno, entrepreneur couple,
Affinity Force International Corporation, CA

"What I love most about this book is the way Anolia shared her life experiences as well as what her family struggled with. Thank you very much for empowering me through this book. This book made me realize that whatever I'm going through financially I'm not alone and 'this too shall pass.' Thank you Anolia and keep on inspiring a lot of people!"
M. Rayo, entrepreneur, CA

Leah's short talk this evening was as effective and inspiring as a hundred personal growth seminars strung together, back to back. Leah draws you in, with her genuine warmth and caring to impart a deep and personal wisdom that resonates with everyone blessed enough to hear her.
L. Farrar, entrepreneur, CA

Yes! the SECRETS WORK

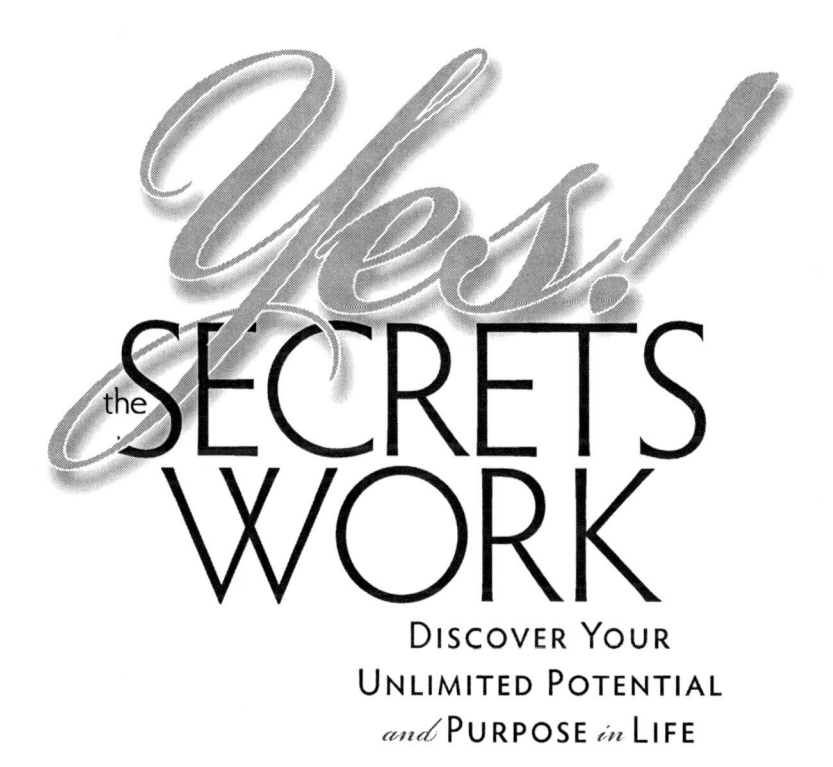

Discover Your Unlimited Potential *and* Purpose *in* Life

Anolia Orfrecio Facun

New York

Yes! The Secrets Work!

Copyright 2009© Anolia Orfrecio Facun. All rights reserved.
No part of this publication may be reproduced or transmitted in any form or by any means, mechanical or electronic, including photocopying and recording, or by any information storage and retrieval system, without permission in writing from the author or publisher (except by a reviewer, who may quote brief passages and/or short brief video clips in a review.)

Disclaimer: The Publisher and the Author make no representations or warranties with respect to the accuracy or completeness of the contents of this work and specifically disclaim all warranties, including without limitation warranties of fitness for a particular purpose. No warranty may be created or extended by sales or promotional materials. The advice and strategies contained herein may not be suitable for every situation. This work is sold with the understanding that the Publisher is not engaged in rendering legal, accounting, or other professional services. If professional assistance is required, the services of a competent professional person should be sought. Neither the Publisher nor the Author shall be liable for damages arising herefrom. The fact that an organization or website is referred to in this work as a citation and/or a potential source of further information does not mean that the Author or the Publisher endorses the information the organization or website may provide or recommendations it may make. Further, readers should be aware that internet websites listed in this work may have changed or disappeared between when this work was written and when it is read.

All Scripture quotations are taken from *The New King James Version* / Thomas Nelson Publishers, Nashville: Thomas Nelson Publishers. Copyright © 1982. Used by permission. All rights reserved.

This book is designed to provide accurate and authoritative information with regard to the subject matter covered. This information is given with the understanding that neither the author nor the publisher is engaged in rendering legal, professional advice. Since the details of your situation are fact dependent, you should additionally seek the services of a competent professional.

ISBN 978-1-60037-627-6

Library of Congress Control Number: 2009925284

MORGAN · JAMES
THE ENTREPRENEURIAL PUBLISHER

Morgan James Publishing, LLC
1225 Franklin Ave., STE 325
Garden City, NY 11530-1693
Toll Free 800-485-4943
www.MorganJamesPublishing.com

Habitat for Humanity®
Peninsula
Building Partner

In an effort to support local communities, raise awareness and funds, Morgan James Publishing donates one percent of all book sales for the life of each book to Habitat for Humanity. Get involved today, visit www.HelpHabitatForHumanity.org.

Dedication

This book is dedicated to:

Our *God,* who loves us so much and through whom nothing is impossible.

My *family*, my loving husband, *Victor,* and our three wonderful children, *Cristern, Grace Ann,* and *Genesa,* who gave me their unconditional love and full support, which helped me survive life, live to the fullest, and finish this book.

Our *parents, teachers* and *leaders,* for you bear great responsibilities for the lives that you touch and impact each day. My sincere hope is that even just a portion of this book will be of help or support to you in your role. We are very grateful to you.

All of *you,* whom God loves so much, are my greatest motivation to complete this book. This one is for *you…*

Acknowledgement

First, and foremost, I would like to acknowledge *you* for choosing to read this book, for desiring to discover your best self and the best that you still can be. Waiting for you to experience now are the fulfillment of your dreams and greatest desires in life. My best wishes to you.

I would also like to take this opportunity to express my deepest appreciation to the following special people and leaders who have touched so many lives, including mine. They have contributed tremendously to my search for and discovery of myself and what this life, this world is all about.

Art and Angela Williams – the first and the greatest leaders my husband and I have known in our lives. Their courage, integrity, and leadership of A.L. Williams Corporation, now known as Primerica Financial Services, have fostered many great leaders and successful companies of our time.

Rick Warren, Joel Osteen, Dick Bernal, Michael Pitts, Adam Bernal – God truly anointed them, and each is living his calling. Their words and encouragement were there for me when I needed them most. Their books helped me discover more of myself and my purpose.

To Earl Nightingale, Napoleon Hill, Zig Ziglar, Bryan Tracy, Denis Waitley, Wayne Dyer, Robert Kiyosaki, Jay Abraham, Michael Gerber, Vic Conant, and the rest of the Nightingale–Conant Corporation authors who introduced me to a wealth of knowledge that I desperately needed. To this day these wonderful, successful people continue to share a wealth of information to many.

Anthony Robbins – for being a living example of a transformed life, from rags to riches, who helped many people move from ordinary to extraordinary, being the best they can be.

Bob Proctor and his dynamic *SGR Team, Mark Victor Hansen and distinguished guests* – for the most incredible seminar cruise they put together in 2007. The like-minded people I had the pleasure and privilege of meeting and networking with were all amazing individuals. That cruise totally pushed me to fulfill my dreams, visions, and destined purpose.

And to many more *authors* and *speakers* whose books, taped messages, and seminar speeches successfully helped me to find myself and the power to transform my life and be the best that I can be. My sincerest gratitude that someday I will also be able to contribute to those individuals I was purposely created for. Without these wonderful human beings, this book would not be possible. I highly recommend that you grab the opportunity to read or listen to the works of those I have acknowledged in this book, because *the secrets are for you, too.*

Last but not the least, to *Virginette Acacio, Glo Bernales Madarang, Madelena Montiel, Cheryl Valk, Russell Ramos, James Ramos,* and *Diana Liffengren,* for their support, devoting enormous time reviewing, and whose sensitive editing added clarity to this book's message; to *Rick Frishman, David Hancock, Jim Howard* and *Margo Toulouse* of Morgan James Publishing, for the incredible support they have extended; and to *Rachel Lozez* and *George Snyder* for the cover and interior book design. Yes! The Secrets Work! would not been possible without their support.

Table of Contents

Introduction	**xiii**
The Secrets	**1**
What Secrets?	1
Discover the Real You!	2
My Personal Self-Discovery	4
You are Wonderfully Created, Marvelously Unique	7
The Truth Can Set You Free (at Last)!	8
The Secrets to Total Wellness	**11**
Yes, You Can Be Happy, Healthy, and Prosperous	11
Physical Health	19
Mental Health	21
Emotional Health	25
Spiritual Health	27
Social Health	38
Financial Health	39
Health Balance and Priorities	47
Understanding the Secrets of Life	**51**
The Way of Life	52
Life as a Puzzle	56

The Secrets of Survival — 61

Facing Tough Times: My Personal Survival Story — 62
Being Homeless — 62
Mistakes and Failures are Helpful — 71
Overcoming Handicaps and Disabilities — 74
The Problem Solving Process — 76
The Dream Achievement Process — 82

The Secrets of the Wealthy — 85

Three Ways to Make Money — 85
Rule of 72 — 87
Three Types of People — 93
Life will Give You What You will Take — 94

The Secrets to a Joyful and Meaningful Life — 97

Life's ABCs — 97
Learn to Live with a Song — 102
Learn to Live with a Motto — 103
Morals and Family Values are Vital — 106

Now, What's Next? — 111

The Key is Within You — 111
A Shared Vision — 118
Together Making a Difference — 120

A Final Note from the Author	125
Individuals, Groups, and Organizations Making a Difference	**127**
Book of Life Reference List	**131**
Declaration	**133**
DO IT ANYWAY	135
About the Author	137
Free Bonus Gifts	139
Emergency Contact Numbers And Other Resources	140

Introduction

YES! Just the sound of it is like music to your ears. Yes, in this book, you are about to make your greatest discovery: *your life, yourself!* How magnificent life is! Life is good and beautiful. Regardless of the way we feel, life can be meaningful and fruitful. Together, through this book, we can begin to re-discover what life really is all about and what makes it worth living to the fullest. I desire that by the time you finish reading this book, you will find yourself more equipped to deal with the present and the future.

Yes! The Secrets Work! is a timely and practical book written to bring *light* to life, *truth* to set us free, and *hope* to help us go on. It hopes to bring comfort and encouragement to those who feel depressed, stressed, lonely, or empty; courage to those who fear; hope to those who feel hopeless; and strength to those who feel weak or that they can't go on. It hopes to bring healing to those who are feeling ill and peace to those longing to forgive or be forgiven. It hopes to reach those individuals looking for answers: *youth* needing more guidance; *adults* seeking hope in the midst of their broken dreams; and *seniors* searching for a reason to keep on living and a way to make their final contributions.

In order to accomplish this, I tell it like it is. No fancy words, but plain, simple, practical, and useful words, so that you may gain insight right away as you read along. For your part, you must keep a total *open mind*, ready to absorb, examine, or consider what you are about to discover. A great portion of what you will learn or discover is not commonly taught in our schools. The information is vital, but amazingly only a very small fraction of the population has access to these valuable secrets. These few individuals either have someone in their circle of family and friends who passed on the valuable information, or they are like me, who had to spend over twenty years and tens of thousands of dollars to gain this treasured knowledge. I feel compelled to share these great secrets that can significantly transform lives, and for the mere cost of a book.

My personal search and discovery started when I was in my twenties when my husband and I realized that even though we were both professionals, we did not know everything, especially on financial area. I was missing out on so much valuable information out there, and even now, I feel I still have so much to learn. I must be on the slow side because it took me too long to figure out how to put together all the pieces of puzzle that make up *life*. It is a wonderful, "I got it!" feeling to see the picture of my life in the making. There are still a few pieces left to complete the picture of my life, my purpose, but I am now more assured than ever, in spite of all the complexities and challenges that I may still go through, that everything is going to be all right.

Now, how about you? How are you doing with your path through life? Remember that each of us is a story to be told, a masterpiece canvass picture to be shared, which sooner or later could be a song to be played or a movie to be watched. Isn't that interesting? If you knew this earlier, could you have done a better job? How do you want your life story to read?

Don't you worry, my friend. Everything will be all right for you, too. I have poured out everything that I have learned and experienced with all the interesting people I have met in life into this book. This is with a hope that you will learn the secrets, figure out things, and be more equipped in life with less time, less expense, and hopefully less pain and agony than I experienced. If only I knew then what I know now…

Remember, I can neither provide nor guarantee success. It is entirely up to *you* to do the work that will get you to the end of the rainbow to discover your own treasure. It will be quite an adventure. I can assure you that you will not get there overnight, but if you have the right mindset, it will be an exciting journey. And when the time comes that suddenly you can say, "I get it!" "Yes! I got it!" I can assure you, you will also be one of the happiest people alive on this planet!

In reality your journey through life involves creating strategic plans to tackle the obstacles and challenges along the way. Remember, the goal is for you to reach your destination successfully and to come out winning in life—*happy, joyful, healthy, wealthy, and fulfilled in every aspect of your life.*

How do you do that? Are you *ready* for answers? Then let's begin…

Yes! The *good news* is: *life* can still be different, exciting, and meaningful! It can still be better for each of us, for all of us. Don't let anything or anyone stop you on your road to discovery. Don't let any negative thoughts tell you that you can't, that it is impossible…because *you can*! And anything is *possible*!

The Secrets

What Secrets?

Yes! What once was secret is no longer secret. When you go to the Internet or a bookstore, you will find hundreds of titles referring to "the secret"…the secret to this and that …of everything under the sun. What is a secret anyway? According to Webster's New World Dictionary, *secret* means: "keeping from the knowledge of others, beyond general knowledge or understanding, hidden, something not revealed, understood, or explained, mystery." Hmm…

In this book then, we will uncover, reveal, find, and make known, and together we will solve the mystery of *the secrets*. At this point, I would like to personally congratulate and express my great appreciation to Rhonda Byrne, author of the phenomenal bestseller book and movie *The Secret*, together with the carefully selected speakers, authors, and teachers involved who all did a magnificent job of heightening awareness to the law of attraction. Finally, this longtime secret is now readily available to the general public. Byrne paved the way for *Yes! The Secrets Work!* The law of attraction once again proved to work, as she did the difficult part of the search and exposure of this longtime hidden secret. My intent is not to reinvent the wheel or try to surpass what was already marvelously put together but to embrace the good impact it can bring to more people—to reinforce, to reaffirm that these secrets, when discovered, believed, and applied, truly create wonders.

If you have read or viewed *The Secret*, understand that there are other secrets still left for you to uncover. Life (and the secrets to success in life) is much more than the law of attraction. Again, are you *ready*? Let's begin…

First, let's mention here *the greatest disaster of all time:* I believe that the greatest disaster and most terrible waste of all time is that there are people who have lived their lives without even knowing their potential.

Sad to say, many people nowadays merely *exist* rather than *live*. Can this be corrected or improved?

It is then very important that we start with *you,* my friend. Wouldn't you like to know who you really are, your potential? Wouldn't it be great to discover and develop your hidden gifts, natural talents, and abilities? These potentials, especially given to or designed for you, when discovered and utilized, can help you not only to survive in this life but to live and experience your life to the fullest. Yes! Isn't it time that you discover more secrets about *you*?

Discover the Real You!

Do you know who you really are? The real *you*? When possible, I want you to go in front of the mirror and look at yourself. Now, can you tell who you are by what you see in that mirror? Do you like what you see? Do you like the person facing you? Who is that anyway? Is that really *you*? No, I am not just talking about the face or body that you can see. Now, look again. Move closer to the mirror. (If you have not done it yet, you will really appreciate this important exercise more if you get up and actually go stand in front of the mirror.)

Let's do this again. Ready? Now, move closer to the mirror. It's like being face-to-face with someone. What do you see? You are now face-to-face with the hidden *you*. What am I talking about? Look at your *eyes*. Are you beginning to have a conversation with somebody there? (Go ahead.) Next, *smile!* Yes, please, just follow along, because this will be an interesting exercise. Remember, you are trying to make a discovery here, maybe one of the greatest discoveries you will ever make, if not the most important, long overdue discovery. Again, *smile* the best, most beautiful smile you have. Is the person you are facing happy?

For a moment focus on looking at your eyes; continue looking if there's a conversation happening. Eventually you will notice that the way you perceive or see yourself seems to be changing somehow. Now, make faces, all kinds of faces; have fun with yourself or the inner you; laugh if you want. It is okay. The more you get acquainted and comfortable with the *inner you*, the stronger and better the person you will become. Why? Because you will not be like people who merely exist or are like walking zombies, those who look like lifeless physical bodies, looking or feeling *empty* inside. It is because you will begin to have a more in-depth understanding of your *whole being*. You will begin to discover the *total you*. The *real you* will not only be a physical body but also a spirit, a mind, and a full range of emotions as well. You will be a person who continuously relates with others and the universe. *You* are not just muscles and bones, face and color, cells and DNA, and all these physical things that can be looked at, tested, and examined. *You* are a lot more than that.

As we go along, you will discover unseen, undiscovered, and difficult-to-explain phenomena. The good thing is that there are many enthusiastic scientists who have done research to unfold and provide scientific explanations for the phenomena mentioned in the book *The Secret* that have benefited many known and great people in our history. We do appreciate our scientists who dedicated time and effort to finding answers and explanations and have satisfied our curious minds.

Let's pause and ponder for a moment. Did you make a discovery in the mirror? Did you discover the inner *you*, the one who is beyond the physical body and face that you and the others can see? If you did, that is great! If you don't know what I am talking about at this point, just read on and try to do the exercise again later.

Examine this simple formula:

What You Think → You Feel → You Manifest or Realize.

Let's do another exercise. If you really want to learn and master *the secrets* about you, and you really want to get good results out of this, then first follow these simple instructions and put this formula to the test.

First, *think* that you are sad, or think of something that makes you sad. Do you *feel* sadness? Look at the mirror. What do you see? Do you look sad? What happens when you are sad? Just because you *thought* of sadness, almost instantly you *feel* it, and suddenly sadness is *manifesting* itself in your face and slumped body.

Now, *think* that you are *happy*! Think of something that makes you happy. Look at the mirror. Do you feel and look happy? Did you notice that you have a smile on your face, your body is straighter, and you look much better? Peter Pan has to think of happy thoughts to be able to fly. In the same way that actors simply have to think and feel their roles, they can switch from crying to laughing any time. Sports players, especially boxers, and other performers have to condition their minds before going into the arena. If not, they will get knocked down right away. You set your mind on what you want to accomplish, and the feeling that follows will spring you into action, to manifesting or realizing your desires. It's that simple. So, keep thinking good thoughts.

The real you is more beautiful and capable, is bigger and stronger than what you physically see in that mirror. What is inside you needs to be discovered, recognized, acknowledged, and nurtured in order for you to become the best you can be, in order for you to reach your fullest potential. Your life, once again, can be even more meaningful and exciting when you recognize that you are not limited by what you can see in the mirror but rather by what you can *see in your mind* and *feel in your heart*. You will only look like a winner when you have the mind and the heart of a champion. You will discover that you, your universe, and your potential truly are unlimited! All you need now is to *believe*, to *act* on what you believe, and to live your life to the fullest. Then you will see your goals accomplished, your dreams realized. You will be at *peace* with yourself and with others. You will experience true *joy*. This healthy state of mind and emotion will keep you in the best health…which already makes you, not just rich, but wealthy in every way! Having all that is living… *abundant living*.

Hold on. You are not done yet. In fact, this is just the beginning. It will get more exciting as we go along. Now, let me share some insights through…

My Personal Self-Discovery

I remember Leah (my nickname) as a happy little girl, but as she began to go to school and be exposed with children in her surroundings, she developed such an inferiority complex. She was abnormally tall for a girl in her country, so she was a sure target of constant ridicule. How she overcame that inferiority was a miracle, mainly through other people who cared. She reached and finished college with a bachelor of science in nursing degree from a well known and wonderful school that taught her a lot about life, God, and true service for and fellowship of mankind. She continued to explore more great discoveries when she came to America at the tender age of twenty-two. Her natural adventurous spirit and curiosity for anything and everything helped her continuously acquire valuable information from various fields, not only in her profession but in other industries and aspects of life like business, finance, real estate, etc. She was not afraid to put things to test, to validate the information. Actual experiences are her greatest teachers. As she gained more knowledge and experience that were beneficial, it was natural for her to share these to others so they, too, could benefit. Her passion has always been public health education. She also has been an active volunteer in her church, her children's schools, and the communities wherever her family is residing. Some of the projects she participated in or initiated are: parents' classes, tree planting, emergency and disaster preparedness, walk for youth, making a difference day projects, etc. Yes! The more talents and abilities she continued to discover, the happier she became, because she felt she could share and help others even more.

It is truly interesting to watch myself grow and develop to what I am now. Although I have read countless books in my life, attended so many seminars and personal and business development workshops (and booth camps), what helped me most in my self-discovery is what I call the "Book of Life." It is referred to by many as the Bible, but I see too many books at bookstores and libraries using that title on "everything you need to know" or "how-to" type of books, so for my own differentiation I will call it the Book of Life or the Living Word. And that is a well-fitting name because, of the many books that I have read, this one has such distinction in providing answers to the questions I have about LIFE, such as better understanding of my life and the lives of others and how to best live life in this very complex and challenging world of ours. I found this book to be like a complete library with answers to every question I have. Everything is in this amazing book. I used to ask myself, "How could one modestly-sized book cover everything from the beginning to the end of this world, from the time I was conceived to my final destiny? How could it cover everything from the way I should live my life to how to build relationships to how to be healthy, happy, and successful in life?" I don't ask anymore. I just know that when I am seeking an answer, this amazing book will deliver. It also helped me understand that I, like everyone else who will pass this earth, will go through life's many tests, trials, and tribulations. Yet it has also given me great comfort and insights not only on how to deal with these challenges as they come up, but also on how to come out victorious.

I have to give the Book of Life the full credit because I once came to a realization that, as a human, I have my weaknesses and limits. I have to admit that life is sometimes too tough, more than I can bear, but the knowledge that I am not just an insignificant human being and the comfort that I get from God's promises to His people, His children, and to me have helped me press on in those times when I most needed help. I could have given up long ago, numerous times, but this book kept me going. It taught me and helped me to never give up. I am truly grateful for this. Can you imagine if I had missed out on all the wonderful things I have experienced later after the deadly hurricanes of my life were over? I would have missed out on the beautiful endings ahead of me, living my life's purpose according to God's master plan.

Nowadays, more and more people are finding life to be too tough or too stressful to live, and at times it could be too lonely out there. After my long journey through life, having my own fair share of life's ups and downs and witnessing many people from all walks of life out there, I have concluded: more than ever, *"People need to connect with God."* God, also referred to as the Higher Power or the Most High, is the ultimate answer, the One who can provide the ways and means for everything we need in this life. The Book of Life is the main connection we have to get to know God better, His ways and His marvelous love for each of us, for all of us.

I also have to give credit to so many people and groups: true friends, churches who cared and those special people, groups, and companies that I acknowledged at the beginning and will acknowledge at the end portion of this book, who all gave me and my family the support we needed and allowed me to witness, verify, and experience the truth and reality of the Book of Life. I have also found it amazing that the nuggets of wisdom, the quotes, the stories, and sayings that I heard from the elders of my youth are all based on this book. If you already have this book, then you know what I am talking about. If you have one and have not opened it yet or if you have no copy of this book, then get a hold of one and start making your amazing discoveries as you are riding on, surviving, or enjoying your journey through life.

You are Wonderfully Created, Marvelously Unique

Yes! You are not just anybody. You are not just any average and ordinary Jane or Joe. You are not even just special. You are way more than that! Are you aware that:
- Mankind, including you and I, was created in God's image, in His likeness. He even gave man His own breath of life.
- God knew you while you were still being formed.
- God knows you by name, along with everything else about you.
- God knows the very number of your hairs.
- No two individuals are exactly alike. For example, no two individuals have the same fingerprints.

Specially made, yes, that's what each of us is. It became very clear that God has planned for each of us to be part of Him from the very beginning. Of all His creations, we are the only one He created in His own image and gave His own breath of life. When you were being formed in your mother's womb, before you were even born, God already knew you and had plan for you. As I write this portion, I have just made a startling discovery: although some people are fixated or absorbed with the thought that "I am just an accident," when it comes to God, no one is an accident. Does anyone think that a couple making love is also busy thinking of a life being formed during the process? What do you think? This is amazing! Our parents don't think about us or know about us until we are already formed, a few weeks or months later when they get a positive result on the pregnancy test. *Positive!* I particularly like that first word used referring to the new life formed. God, who knows about us from the time we are being conceived or formed, is our true Creator. You were born to be *a plus*, not a minus or to be insignificant. You and I were allowed to come to this earth as *a positive addition* (Remember that!), an asset, *to fulfill a purpose* or *make a contribution*.

Our beloved parents are the blessed vessels provided to bring us into this world and nurture us until we all go back home to our true Father and Creator. When it is your turn to experience what it is like to bring a child into this world, then you will have a better appreciation and love for your given parents. The sooner you can honor, love, and care for your parents, the more blessings will flow to you.

The last point about the unique fingerprint each of us has is to prove to you that each and every one of us is unique. There is nobody else exactly like any one of us. Of the billions of people in this world whose fingerprints have been taken, no two individuals have the same exact fingerprints; not even identical twins are exactly alike or share same fingerprints. Isn't that interesting? Another point is the use of DNA to uniquely identify each of us, which is, of course, more complicated to explain, so we will not even make an attempt to discuss it here. These facts simply prove that it is true how special we are to God, that God can single us out from the rest of the population. Isn't that amazing?

For me personally, what's even greater is my faith and knowledge that the owner of this entire universe who loves us so much is *my Father*, and I am *His child*. The *good news* is: you and anyone else can believe and claim that, too, if you want to. Can you imagine what that makes us? You? I have faith, but I used to get bogged down feeling like nobody at times. But after confirming all these things, I feel more like *a conqueror*. The universe is for us to conquer, according to His will and purpose for us. Are you ready for more?

The Truth Can Set You Free (at Last)!

There is nothing better in life than to be *free*! *Freedom* remains a universal human drive. Unfortunately, a lot of people remain blind or confused about what freedom really means. Do you have real freedom? Freedom implies the absence of hindrance, restraint, confinement, or repression. To be free is wonderful, if it is true freedom. The truth is, freedom is not only *physical* but also *mental, emotional, spiritual, social,* and *financial*. Otherwise it can be just a clever disguise of what actually is a path to destruction. People do a lot of incredible, sometimes even crazy things to attain what they call freedom. What good is it if you are dead, in prison, a fugitive, or living a life of emptiness or misery? Is that freedom? Something is wrong. Someone is lying to you, to us.

The *truth* can set you *free*! Take note that there is a pre-requisite to true freedom, the truth. Even in court, when the truth prevails, the fate of the suspect's freedom or imprisonment can be determined. Imprisoned or not, the true guilty one will still continuously be haunted by the truth. If you really want to live a life with freedom and peace, to live a truly meaningful and victorious life, then seek and embrace the truth. It is unfortunate that we are now living in a world of lies. These lies are designed to distract your attention and divert your focus from the real truth, from what is really good for you. The master deceiver of this world, whose job is to constantly influence people, has only one purpose: to lead people to self-destruction.

The evil master, or the *thief*, of this world is cunning and manipulative. It is so good at giving negative or destructive suggestions that they are almost unnoticeable. It uses people and circumstances. It knows your weaknesses. It knows exactly how, where, and when to attack in such a subtle way that, most of the time, you will not know that your situation is its doing until it is too late. Remember that this evil manipulator does not care about you at all, but it is so good at pretending it does. In the end, it laughs at people's foolishness for the destruction it has caused. It always has; it always will. The Book of Life says *"We do not wrestle against flesh and blood, but against principalities, against powers, against the rulers of the darkness of this age..."* If you do not know what I am talking about, open your eyes and find out more about it, for it is real. It is reality. (You will find the Book of Life reference at the end portion of this book).

Either that same liar masters your life and wins in bringing you to destruction, or you stand firm and reclaim your life and the beautiful things that it is trying to steal from you. Win the battle and live the abundant life that you ought to have. The Book of Life says, *"The thief does not come except to steal and to kill and to destroy…"* Suicide, homicide, and divorce are just three of the undesirable results that rob us of our dreams and joy. But the Lord says, *"I have come that you may have life and that you may have it more abundantly."* If we were meant to have an ABUNDANT (joyful, fulfilled, victorious) life, what is blocking our way from experiencing it? Why are there people who are unhappy, pressured on all sides, trapped, and in bondage? Consider this for a moment. Do you have the truth that can set you free?

The Secrets to Total Wellness

> *"Most people are about as happy as they make up their minds to be."*
> Abraham Lincoln, sixteenth president of the
> United States of America

Yes, You Can Be Happy, Healthy, and Prosperous

You may have all the money in the world, but what is it for if you are not healthy and happy? *Health is wealth* and is a source of happiness.

But what is *happiness* anyway? Is it being in this age of ultra modern technology that aims to gain us access to all comfort and conveniences; where everything we need and want are supposedly available? Ironically, *happiness* is a word still highly sought after, remaining on many peoples' lists as still *undiscovered* and *unrealized*.

People naturally have various definitions of what happiness is. To some it is having everything they have ever *wanted*. To others it is simply having everything they have ever *needed*. And still to others it is everything they ever *wished* for. We all, of course, have different ideas as to what we want, need, or wish.

Since I have found that most people believe *being healthy* brings happiness, we will start there. If health brings happiness, and being happy is definitely healthy, then this cycle puts us on the right track. By the way, do you know that experts on success have found that a healthy, happy person has a better chance to succeed? That should not be surprising.

So, just what does *healthy* really mean? Some people think that if they just stick to their ideal weight, that's healthy. In America people spend billions of dollars yearly in search of the perfect, healthy, beautiful body. People buy expensive machines and gadgets to exercise and stay fit or attend spas and clinics to stay young and beautiful. But why is it then, that there are countless numbers of successful businessmen, movie stars, athletes, wealthy men, and gorgeous women who have everything that money can buy but are still lonely, empty, and miserable? I do not need to name them. We read about them in newspapers and see them on TV every day. Some become involved in drugs, some go through painful divorces, and others commit suicide. It is sad. What has happened to them?

Over the years I have come to this conclusion: when people are healthy, they are happy. People who are experiencing some sort of health problems are unhappy. If the health problem is not resolved, it makes the person more susceptible to more problems or unhappy situations. So…

How do we know when someone is not totally well?

Let's take this simple test again and gauge for a moment your knowledge of *health* and *total well-being*. Check the items you believe are signs and symptoms of health problems.

____elevated or abnormal temperature

____difficulty of breathing

____persistent chest discomfort/pain

____not eating or overeating

____smoking

____drunkenness

____exhibiting obscene or violent behaviors

____compulsive gambling

____drug use

____can't seem to think straight, very distracted or disturbed

____worrying too much or always afraid

____feeling so stressed out or burned out

____depressed for a long period of time

This should be an easy test, right? How many people actually realize that each and every one of these are signs or symptoms of health problems? In fact, these are but a few of a very long list of signs and symptoms indicative of an *unhealthy state* of a person. The overall number and severity of symptoms in turn become a reflection of the health status of *a society*.

Symptoms like fever, breathing difficulties, or severe pain can easily tell us that *something is wrong* and can alarm us enough to seek a doctor or go to a hospital. On the other hand, there are some people who do not realize their symptoms and who are likely to deny that they have any health problems at all. When I see someone smoking, I do not just see a person who is a candidate for lung cancer. The main thing that comes to my mind is, "There must be a reason why this person has to smoke."

If you or someone you know who comes to mind right now happen to exhibit any of the symptoms on the list (regardless of number), it is time for some *self-evaluation*. As you progress in this book, you'll be better able to identify specific problems and needs, possible sources or factors affecting a person, and what can be done about them. Depending on the mildness or severity of the problem, coping ability, and available resources of help, one may be able to resolve the problem on his/her own, or one may need to seek professional help, or a combination of the two. Still the *decision* and determination to recover from any health problem rests mainly on the individual.

Two current pressing health issues are:

Obesity and Eating Disorders: It is quite interesting that while *malnutrition* is a great problem in other countries, in America, referred to as "the land of excess," the statistics show that *obesity* is of great concern for many people, including our youth. The health problems associated with obesity, including hypertension, diabetes, and heart diseases have not only physical effects, but most often also mental, emotional, social, and financial impact on individuals with an obesity problem. We can also add to these issues the inadequate nutritional information and weight loss obsession, especially among our younger generation, which has caused *eating disorders* to become more prevalent. Incidentally these health challenges also put huge financial burden on our already crippled government healthcare system and budget. Are there solutions and preventive measures for these problems? The answer is yes!

Family Problems: This second one is also a social issue that has great impact on the overall health of, not just the couple, but the entire family. It is a known fact that there are more separated or divorced couples than there are married couples staying together nowadays. Divorce puts physical and financial strain on the whole family, but more concern should be directed toward the mental and emotional impact on our children, who are being exposed to unstable family environments. At times these children are ending up displaced or disassociated from a much needed nurturing environment. Can more of these situations possibly be prevented?

Let me share with you some basic information I have incorporated into my individual and group health teachings. You may find it helpful for yourself personally or someone else. It is nothing new; it is just not well known or applied.

How do we attain health to be happy?

Being a nurse has been a great advantage for me. I learned early what health really meant and how to attain it. It means *being well* or a state of *well-being*, simple words with very broad, complex meanings. As I share with you the true nature of *health and well-being*, you will find that it is not just about ideal body weight or a good diet or even a terrific fitness program. It is a lot more than just that.

As a nurse I learned that when I took care of a patient, I was not only to care for the broken leg or burned arm, fever or pain. I had to care for an individual's PHYSICAL, MENTAL, EMOTIONAL, SPIRITUAL and SOCIAL WELL-BEING as well.

For example, a football player comes to a hospital for a serious spinal injury. While the medical staff's initial priority is to stabilize his physical condition, their next immediate consideration is the mental and emotional impact of his condition. Furthermore, there are the social considerations and spiritual counseling if so desired. For someone who is not that strong and who is left alone, the situation can be devastating. At this time, family and friends are usually the best sources of support for him. They are the major factors influencing his speedy recovery.

Let it be known that an individual is made up of integrated parts that cannot be separated from one another nor ignored nor disregarded. Each of those parts is *uniquely important* and has to be considered as an inseparable part of one's *whole being*. That is why when we focus on just one or two of those parts, we usually end up feeling that we are missing something. We feel that our life is *not complete*. We can always tell when we are not completely well, or not *all together*. This is when we need to realize that we are in need of a self check-up.

As I also became aware of how tremendously our economic or financial situations affect us, I added another very important aspect to my view of life and well-being. I modified my definition of *health* as *"to care for and to meet an individual's needs for his/her physical, mental, emotional, spiritual, social, and financial total well-being."* Does one really have to wait until he becomes a patient for his whole being to be considered? Why was I not aware of this concept until I was midway into college? Realizing that not too many people understand this concept of *whole being*, it is too important to disregard. So I will pass it on to you now…

It is quite unfortunate that we are living in a very *physically oriented* society. If you ask our young students about what our basic needs are, their automatic response will be "food, shelter, and clothing." As these children grow up and become adults like us, they tend to focus more on the food they eat, where they will live, and shopping for the things they want to wear. Along with that is the remarkable obsession for a beautiful body or anything else "nice to look at." These adolescents will become caught up in the disillusion that these are the most important needs in life. But this is a big misconception. They will eventually come to realize that they are missing out on a lot of things or are sacrificing things that are really important. Let me try to explain:

Let us look at a typical individual and understand how he can bring his integrated parts *together* to meet all his needs so he can be *happy* and *healthy*. Here are the parts:

- Physical – what you see that is obvious; your body and its desires.

- Mental – centered in your brain; your mind, intellect, reasoning, and way of thinking.
- Emotional – your emotions or feelings; associated with the heart as the center of our emotion because of the way it is affected as it pounds when we are afraid, angry, excited, or in love.
- Spiritual – you cannot see it, but you know it is there; your inner being, your conscience (of what is right and what is wrong).
- Social – those surrounding you; those you associate with and build relationships with; family, friends, etc.
- Financial – your pocket book; your checkbook balance, assets, and other money matters.

Here is an illustration. Let's take a single young woman who finds herself attracted to a very handsome man. One day she discovers herself battling within. Her *physical* side is definitely attracted to how good looking he is. He is very sexy, and she may begin to imagine herself in his arms. Her easy-to-persuade *emotions* may convince her that she is in love with this guy with all of her heart, mind, and soul. If she is still with her senses, her more practical *mental* part may intercede and say, "Wait a minute! Are you crazy? How could you be attracted to, much more be in love with, a guy who probably has no education, no future, no penny to his name? You don't even have any idea where he came from." Her *financial* side will interject, "If he cannot feed you, how will you feed him?" And her *spiritual* side may suggest, "Before you do anything, at least check his background, his character, values, and beliefs. Is he married, or does he have other girlfriends? Can you live with that?" Depending on what kind of friends she has, her *social* side can affect her choices as well. So you see how easily some girls can be carried away, while others will take the time to weigh everything first and save themselves a lot of grief later.

Another example is on impulsive buying. The *physical* side says, "I like that dress!" The *emotions* will immediately agree that, "It will feel wonderful to wear it." The *mental* part will try to intercede, saying, "You have so many clothes already; you don't need it." The *financial* side will most likely agree. And the *spirit* will add, "Use your money wisely." These examples are typical of what happens to us practically every minute of the day.

You see, in our physically driven society, it is so easy for anyone to like what they see, jump into it, and realize later that they made a big mistake. If they had *only given it some thought*, it would have prevented them from unnecessary pain and regrets. The truth is, it actually takes only a few moments of your precious time to realize that you have *other parts* that need to be considered and listened to. Instead of just listening to your body or your emotions, learn to *listen to your whole being*. Just as in a boardroom, each member has to be given a chance to share his/her views. A *decision* is then made according to what will best benefit everyone involved in that *one body*. The feet, as another example, cannot just decide to walk and jump over the bridge without recognizing that they are carrying and involving the rest of the whole body.

Unless all inputs are considered (as in all areas of our lives) in the decision-making, the final result can be chaos. Blaming does not help much to correct the situation. In the end, not just one or two parts suffer, but the *whole person* is affected and suffers the consequences. Take society, for example. It is a whole big earth, and yet one man's action or one country's action, without consideration for the others, has an impact on everybody involved whether we are immediately aware of the action or the consequences.

Practical Health Tips:

- *Prevention* is the best medicine. Preventive measures are better than curative measures. It takes less time, money, effort, pain, and agony to prevent an illness or solve a problem than to go to the hospital and be sick in bed. Learn how to stay healthy or be totally well in the first place.
- Learn *balance* and *priorities* for your *whole* well-being. When we take a bath, we do not just clean our face, but we bathe our whole body, right? Just like our car. Washing it is not enough. We make sure it has gas, is tuned up, has air in the tires, etc.; otherwise it might easily break down. In the same way, we need to recognize that *all* our parts are important. You have to make the effort so that the needs of each of your six areas in life

are considered and properly met to attain *balanced health*. The best priorities in life, which I have heard before and apply to my own life and so can testify to their working best, are as follows:

God first.
Family second.
Others third. (This could be other people, career, business, etc.)

- Learn to *meet the needs of each* of your parts for a healthy whole being.
- I am an avid advocate of *nature walks* and/or relaxing *breaks or vacations*. It is healthy. It gives you the break for your mind, body, and spirit to rejuvenate. It is always interesting to see other places, meet different peoples and cultures.
- Be an *informed consumer*. There is a lot of information available in your local library or bookstore regarding total wellness and illness prevention. Included here are being aware of natural cures vs. aggressive medical interventions; natural food supplements vs. prescribed medicines. When prescribed with a medication, treatment, or procedure by your doctor, do not hesitate to *ask* him/her to explain to you why it is needed or how it can help you. What are the possible side effects? Are there other alternatives? As an example, keeping myself abreast with the latest health issues, I encountered a TV show that you might have seen. Out of curiosity, I ordered a book by Kevin Trudeau titled *Natural Cures*, which I not only found interesting, but it opened my eyes to research more on some of the topics mentioned, especially on powerful antioxidants and other natural discoveries that boost our immune systems to maintain health. And this is just one book or example. For your health's sake, do yourself a favor, be informed. Just because of that desire to learn, I have never been as healthy as I am now.

Physical Health

To be physically healthy, the following are very important:

1. Food – Learn *moderation* and *variety* with each meal and snack. Have equal portions of *proteins*, the body building food (meats, poultry, seafood, nuts, beans, etc.); *carbohydrates*, the energy giving food (rice, cereal, potatoes, bread, etc.); *vitamins* and *mineral sources*, the body and immune system booster or disease and illness prevention food (mainly vegetables, fruits and supplements).

Eat more fresh fruits and vegetables. The more *fresh* and *natural* the food, the more nutrients you can get. Try to stay away from processed food, which has little or no nutrients left but only extra calories that can give you unnecessary extra pounds, especially white sugar, salt, and bleached flour. If at all possible, use honey, sea salt, and whole grains instead. Food supplements in more natural form are better than chemically-based food supplements.

How much food? That depends on your build, activities, and health conditions. *Learn to listen to your body.* It will tell you. Do not let your emotions dictate the amount that you should eat. Be as consistent as possible. It is not good to skip meals.

Note: When you are told by your doctor that you have a terminal disease, don't panic. Remember, illnesses and their remedies are not only physically related. You may want to consider a second opinion and/or alternative remedies. It could be as simple as a nutritional approach, which has already helped many people in more comfortable means than invasive approaches. You have to be agreeable and very comfortable with your decision and the medical professionals you will work with to help you win the battle before you allow anything done to you. You are entitled to that.

2. Water – Clean, fresh water is necessary to our proper body functions. It helps facilitate the nourishment of our body cells and the elimination of body wastes and toxins. About six to eight glasses a day is desirable. Drink regularly without having to wait until you feel thirsty. Most of the food we eat naturally contains water. Juice and milk are not substitutes for water but are better than coffee, soda, or other colored drinks. If you are concerned about the quality of the water you are drinking (depending on where you live or in the event of a natural calamity), have it tested or boil your drinking water as necessary.

3. Exercise – Children are naturally active. If not, encourage them to start right now. For us adults, regular exercise is recommended. We vary with our work nature and activities, so learn to listen to your body and what it needs or how much it can take. Walk or be on your feet more than sitting. Be active! This is wonderful to your health, as it improves your circulation and activates your metabolism to burn the calories you've put in. It also helps build your muscles, which naturally burn more calories. Too much can be as bad as too little or nothing at all. Brisk walking, jogging, jumping rope, dancing, or swimming will do well. One does not have to own exercise equipment or have to belong to a gym to exercise and stay fit. If you can afford it and think it will help motivate you more, then go for it. Exercise helps you look your best and feel good about yourself, which in turn helps make you happy and contributes to your overall success.

4. Bathing or Personal hygiene – After a long, tiring day or waking up in the morning to go to work, nothing refreshes us better than a good bath or shower! There is just something magical about it—like a plant under the rain or a car after a car wash. It cleanses and refreshes us. We look, smell, and feel good! Even the motion of bathing provides a simple exercise that improves our circulation. It helps us prevent skin diseases as well.

5. Rest and Relaxation – Take plenty of R&R. This does not mean being lazy, but when you are working hard, long hours, and you are beginning to feel some discomforts (you feel sleepy, burned out, stressed out), it is your body telling you, "Take a break!" Learn to listen to your body. Like a moving car, when the sign says *stop*, you'd better stop or else. When the gas gauge says *empty*, you'd better fill it up. If you want you and your body to get along, to function well and together avoid problems, then do as it suggests. Sleeping six to eight hours per day is recommended. When you are driving or working and you feel sleepy or unable to concentrate, stop. Pull over if you are driving, or shut your eyes if you are working, and give yourself a few minutes to rest. Listening to soothing music, singing, watching children, taking a walk, or simply doing breathing exercises are ways to help you to become calm, relaxed, and rested.

6. Shelter and Clothing – Whoever came up with the idea that food, shelter, and clothing are our three basic needs was only thinking of our physical needs. We are now finding that those are not the only physical needs we have and definitely *not* our whole being's only needs. Amazingly most schools continue to teach those three basic needs to our children. Food, I absolutely agree with. Yes, decent, comfortable shelter and clothing are important to have, but let's face it, we will not just die for lack of them. Today we have a lot of homeless people who have neither a decent place to live nor decent clothes to wear, yet amazingly they are surviving. Clean, comfortable shelter and clothing are desirable and necessary to provide us warmth and privacy. But for us to put so much importance on them, to the point of being buried in debt to have a fancy home or closets of dresses we may never wear, becomes a big problem instead.

You need to distinguish basic needs from extravagance or excess and just plain unnecessary. If you need or really want it and you can afford it, do not deprive yourself. Go for it! Treat yourself sometimes without guilt. If you have some extras, you may find it very gratifying to share them with others less fortunate.

Note: A lot of times our *physical* side needs to be tamed. Both our physical and emotional sides are more concerned with the *present* desires and feelings. What's important to these two is *now*! Learn to recognize that and be quick to balance it with the other parts of your *whole being*.

Mental Health

Are you fascinated about modern technology? The age of computers, network satellites, superhighways, etc., those amazing gadgets, devices, and machines that, we should be reminded, are all *created by man* himself. If these bring you fascination, you should be more amazed at the *brains* that created them! Yet it is unfortunate that until now, with all these wonderful things, mankind remains to have a very limited understanding of how his amazing brain, his *living computer*, functions. All we know is that we have the ability to think and to do things.

Our brain works pretty much like a computer. In fact, a computer is designed to think and function like the most intelligent brain there is. The brain is designed for you to think and respond to your very thoughts and directions. When you say or think sad-things, the message is relayed to your brain, which, through its complex processing, causes your facial muscles to droop down (you look down and out). It may even cause you to have teary eyes. When you say or think happy thoughts, the brain processing causes your facial muscles to feel upbeat or energetic, and a smile automatically radiates from your beautiful face. When you say, "I will do it," the message is again relayed, and amazingly your actions are directed toward *doing* what you said you would do. When you say, "I don't like to do it," then your body does as directed—it does *nothing* until you change its direction.

Actually, whenever we are confronted with a situation, the brain simply translates that to us then waits for our response, what we want to do next. Basically, we *make a choice*: love or hate, fight or flight, attack or forgive, do something or do nothing, etc. Those who create advertising understand this process very well, and it works, doesn't it? They call this human psychology; give a stimulus in such a way that it creates a desirable response.

It is very reassuring to know that within each of us are amazing natural abilities, commonly called *inborn impulses, instincts,* and *reflexes*. These automatically help or protect us at times when there is no time to think. Take time to get to know yourself better. That way you can trust your abilities and your natural instincts even more to make the right choices.

Going back to our powerful brain, remember the computer rule: *garbage in, garbage out*. MENTAL HEALTH means putting the right input into our brains to produce the right results, or output. Think of good things and good things will eventually happen. Feed your brain with good information to produce more productive and satisfying results. A great example to apply this principle is at our common workplaces. Do you or someone you know usually start the day at work with this thought in mind? *Gosh, another day. I'll see my boss and workmates again. I can't stand it!* Sounds familiar? That thought reflects one's attitude the whole day and surely affects both his or her work performance and relationship with others. Learn to reject or delete negative, unproductive thoughts. On the other hand, when you or that someone start the day with gratitude that there's even a job, make a determination that *This will be a great day! I will only focus on giving my best for my assigned task and be understanding and supportive of everyone at work no matter what,* you or anyone will be amazed how that simple, positive, productive thought could significantly impact one's performance and interaction with others. Exercise this principle each day. We'll be creating a happier environment for ourselves and the others.

With continuous practice you will also discover the magic and the wisdom of learning how to *turn negatives into positives.* Be constantly aware of it until you develop the habit. When you begin to feel bad, or negative, lingering on the negatives does not help the situation. Find a reason to count your blessings instead. Think about what you can learn from the situation. Focus on positive, beautiful things. You have a better chance of getting good, positive results and being successful in life.

> *"I keep the telephone of my mind open to peace, harmony, health, love and abundance. Then, whenever doubts, anxiety, or fear try to call me, they keep getting a busy signal – and soon they'll forget my number."*
>
> Edith Armstrong

Here are some more practical tips for Mental Health:

1. Read. Read. Read. – There is still so much to learn. Do not waste your time with junk, useless reading, or just sitting in front of the television. Use your time wisely by reading informative books like how-to books or topics that will be useful in your everyday life. Read about real people, great people, and accomplishments or practical ideas for living a better life.

2. Listen. Listen. Listen. – We share, or *give*, to others when we are talking. If you wish to benefit more, learn to *listen* and *receive*. You can learn from both experts and everyday people. It is amazing how much you can learn from other people's experiences. Their treasures will become your treasures, too.

3. Retain good input only. – Reject and discard bad input and thoughts, such as negative comments people give you, as these don't improve your health. Evaluate. There may be something to positively learn from it. If not, simply shake it off your system. You can learn to do this just like a computer can *delete* and *reprogram*.

4. Exercise your brain. – You will be amazed at its capacity and capabilities. Use your imagination to draw a picture. Write about something of interest, figure out a problem, and experiment with your ideas. Maybe even come out with another great invention or a fantastic idea to help solve some of mankind's problems. Do not limit yourself. I have learned that humans use only ten percent or less of their brain capacity. If that is true, then that is such a waste. On the positive note, can you imagine how much more we can possibly accomplish?

> *"If you want to reach a goal, you must see the reaching in your mind before you actually arrive at your goal."*
>
> Zig Ziglar

I am sure you have heard of the phrase "The sky is the limit!" So, what are you waiting for? Go on, search, research, imagine, discover, create, accomplish something, share, and make a contribution. Be thankful for your wonderful gifts. Utilize them well so that you may find more satisfaction and meaning in life.

So, do you feel young or old? It is not really a matter of age, you know. Are you happy, sad, poor, or rich? Interestingly, the answer is truly just *a state of mind*.

> *"Anybody can do just about anything with himself that he really wants to and makes up his mind to do. We are capable of greater things than we realize."*
>
> Norman Vincent Peale

Emotional Health

Do you feel emotional sometimes? No problem. You are human, and we humans have emotions. What exactly is *emotion*? An emotion is any strong or intense *feeling*, such as love, joy, anger, fear, etc., often accompanied by outward expression or complex bodily reaction. We cannot visibly see it, but we know it is there. We feel it. Haven't you heard or said to someone, "I can see you are sad" or, "My, you are happy today!" or, "It looks like someone is in love." How did you or they know? We don't carry signs with us to announce how we feel, but it is interesting that whatever we feel is well reflected and perceived by others. This is called *body language*. Is what you are saying consistent with what you are showing? Be aware, it shows.

It is very important that we become aware of the way we feel. We have to remind ourselves that we have other parts, which we have to consider, do a constant balance check with. Just like the physical aspect of our being, our emotions tend to be very impulsive. Say a young girl meets a good-looking guy at a party. Just because she felt something unusual or a chemistry going on, that does not mean she is already in love. It is time to think! And it is always wise for her to take a moment to consult with her other integrated parts, or she could do something drastic she may regret later. Checking, thinking about things, and reasoning within oneself can save people a lot of pain and agony.

Going back to our young girl, if she just follows her sudden surge of feeling, saying, "This must be love," and impulsively goes with the guy, she'll forget to even check out who he really is, where he came from, etc., as if those don't matter at the moment. She does not realize that it could be, and most likely it is, a mere lust or a strong physical attraction. In most cases, such emotion immediately fades away as soon as the physical desire is satisfied or gone, followed later by sadness and regret.

Often it is too late to find out much needed information to avoid the undesirable results of an action. Thinking that it was for the sake of experimentation or adventure does not seem to relieve the pain either. This happens a lot among teens, resulting in early or unwanted pregnancies. Those who resort to abortion, thinking it is an easy way out, then live with the guilt and regret for a long time. Those who do not mean to be unfaithful to their spouses end up having lengthy and painful divorces. Those who never thought about the consequences of a single, fleeting moment could find themselves agonizing over a disease they may have contacted. Those few moments could, and have, led to broken relationships, problems affecting health, jobs, and careers, personal finances, and even destroyed reputations beyond repair. In some situations, chains of events lead from one to another, resulting in various addictions, nervous breakdowns, and even suicide.

It sounds ugly, yet these we hear practically every day. One simple, seemingly harmless, wholesome feeling leading to a very unpleasant ending. Who would have even thought of the result? Just because of not taking *a moment to pause, to think, to check*. Other situations result from uncontrolled anger and hate. We hear lots of stories on TV news and in the newspapers involving horrible, violent crimes, including domestic violence. Who is to blame? People tend to point fingers. That is the usual impulse, as if blaming someone or something else could reverse the situation. But blaming does not help. Each of us has to take responsibility for our actions, to be in control of our emotions. Do a check and balance before doing anything; weigh the circumstance and the pros and cons.

Concentrate on absorbing and sharing more constructive emotions like LOVE and JOY. Be aware that emotions like hate, fear, or depression do not do you or anyone else any good. Fear can be deadly. Later we will talk about dealing with fear of the unknown.

Depression is becoming a very serious problem among all ages, from young children to seniors. Depression is a state of excessive sadness or hopelessness, usually with accompanying physical symptoms, associated with loneliness or feeling alone, unworthiness, grief, or finding no hope, no purpose, or meaning in life. Lighten up. It is normal for us humans to feel that way every now and then. We are affected by the weather, our hormones, and certain situations that we deal with every day. Again, you are not alone! Millions of people around you could be depressed also when faced with a mounting pile of bills. It is not the end of the world for you yet.

To better deal with these types of emotion is to divert your attention to something else, like other people or nature. Since I have had plenty of those moments, I can share with you what I have done so far to help myself. I do see and meet people who have sadder circumstance than I had—some with dirty clothes, maybe not even a home. Just by taking off attention to my circumstance and paying attention to other people and things around me, I can easily see that I am more blessed in a lot of ways after all. One day I saw a couple digging in a huge trash bin. Another time I saw a person with no legs on a wheelchair crossing the street, another a blind man with his dog, and yet another a sick lady with all those life-extending gadgets at a hospital unit. As I think about them, I feel I have many more reasons to be thankful. As I pray for those people, I feel energy to get up and do more worthwhile things than just sit or lie there, feeling depressed, doing nothing. Sometimes I go out, go for a walk, look at the trees and their beautiful leaves, hear the birds, or whatever beautiful and positive things that can fill my mind.

Think that while there are people crying, there are people celebrating. While there are people dying, new babies are being born. If you feel depressed, give yourself physical and mental rest. It will help your emotions heal as well. When your brain gets rest, it will be more relaxed and can function better. Going through depressing moments ourselves helps us relate better with others.

Yes, emotions can be mastered and controlled. Who says you cannot have emotions? Emotions can be so beautiful and wonderful that they can lead to something good and useful. Like true love, tested and tried, which can be the most wonderful thing a person can share with someone. Beautiful, more secure children are the result of that. And that makes life go on.

Spiritual Health

Believe it or not, you have a spirit. Just like your emotion, your spirit cannot be visibly seen, but you know it is there. The spirit is probably the most mysterious, least understood part of our lives. It is difficult to explain, and lack of understanding of the spirit makes it disregarded by many.

Let's start with a better understanding of what *spirit* is. Spirit is the essence or force in man, a part of a human being that is incorporeal and invisible and is characterized by will, self-consciousness or personality. This is not just a matter of opinion or theory. It is a fact; each of us, including you and I, has a spirit. Although it is often associated with the mind or intelligence, it should not be confused with the brain or thought processes. It is not just an emotional process either. The spirit is more than that. If the brain is like the motor of the mechanics of the car, the spirit is the very personality or nature of that car (which of course is even more complex to explain). It is evident, though, that it is working closely with all the other parts of our being.

For generations numerous men and women have been confused, misinformed, and disillusioned about their spirituality so that many have avoided this subject. Our world has managed to make the subject so complicated that there are people who just refuse to deal with it. We have to deal with this spiritual matter because our spirit, a vital part of our being, has a need that must be filled for one to attain total, healthy well-being. If we think we can disregard or do without this spiritual side of us, we are only deceiving ourselves. We are just simply exercising a denial process and therefore depriving ourselves of a basic need.

Just like a person must eat food to meet his physical needs; receive intellectual stimulation to meet his mental needs; be loved and cared for to meet his emotional needs; socialize or have meaningful relationship with others to meet his social needs; and work and get paid to meet his financial needs; likewise he also must have a _____ to meet his spiritual need. The blank is for you to fill in and see what answer you will come up with. Go ahead, write your answer in. Is your spirit filled, or it is still blank or empty?

To meet our spiritual need and enjoy spiritual health is really not that difficult or complicated at all. I will be the first to admit that I went through all the stages of misinformation, disillusion, confusion, and apathy before I found the real, simple truth. It took many years of my life to complete my discovery, but I am glad to say that I am now totally free, healthy, and very happy! Once you've found the secret of the true treasures in life, you will have a deeper sense of peace and security, being a complete, whole being.

Let us unveil the simple truth about our spiritual lives. What can fill or meet our spiritual needs? It may surprise quite a number of people to know that the answer to the blank space, to that spiritual vacuum inside us, is not a religion nor a religious belief nor a church affiliation, a doctrine, a fellowship, or any of those sorts of things. So, there is really no such thing as which religion, church, or religious leader is right or wrong or better than the others when it comes to meeting our spiritual need.

While it is important for an individual, and families especially, to go to church to learn more about God and have fellowship with fellow believers, it should be clear that it is the individual's own meaningful *personal relationship with GOD* that ultimately fills and meets his spiritual need. It is that simple. It is not a religion but *a relationship*. As it is not the wedding rituals or what they have or not that count but the *beautiful relationship* that binds the couple together that makes them a happy couple.

You cannot meet your physical needs by just reading a bunch of books about healthy food and a healthy body. You have to actually eat the food, exercise, rest, etc. Right? You actually have to do your part at putting those ideas into a reality. You cannot just daydream about being loved, or you'll wake up empty. It makes a difference when you find real love that fills your heart. You cannot just think or imagine that you are reading all the books in the library and expect to be the smartest kid on the block. You will end up with only that—images of tons of books in the library and nothing else.

In the same way, instead of just thinking that there must be God or just imagining His image, it makes a big difference when you *know* for sure that He is really there. It is a much more meaningful experience to know that God is real in your personal life. *The only reason there are people who do not believe God is because they have not experienced Him yet.* It is hard for people to understand what it is like to be homeless or to relate to the joy of being in Disneyworld unless they have gone through the experience themselves.

If we say that God is not real and that we do not have to bother with each of our spiritual lives, then we are only lying to ourselves, and the truth is not in us. Whether you like it or are aware of it or not, each human being living on this planet has a spiritual side and needs that *only GOD can fill.* Yes, only God can fill that void; that spiritual place in our lives is reserved just for Him, and without Him we will stay empty inside. This emptiness causes us to keep searching and wanting something more. We are not even sure what it is that we are missing. Without God we can surely fill our lives with so many other gods (like money, fame, people, ideas, etc.), and eventually we will discover that these are not enough to fill our emptiness. When we use or hear the phrase, "I am missing something," we must think again. Is it something or *someone*?

The question now is, either one's spirit is submitted to God or submitted to the matters of this world and its master deceiver. That explains why there are good people and there are people who do bad things. Not because some people were born bad. Have you ever seen a newborn baby who is rotten from birth? I know I have not. My longtime experience with both children and adults makes me continue to believe that each of us was created *good* for a *good purpose*. But the master deceiver and destroyer of this world, so far, has been effective at doing its task to deceive, divert attention, destroy individuals, families, and relationships. We know we must fight back, but are we really a match for this powerful monster?

Why God? And why not? He is a Spirit and the very source of life, and only through having a personal relationship with Him can we have victory over the other unseen powers in this world. If we have God with us, who can be against us? Sure, you are entitled to believe it or not. What do you have to lose if you believe anyway? Will it really benefit you more if you do not believe? There will come a point when you will actually have to make that acknowledgement, make a decision whether you really want Him in your life. Seek yourself and find what you really want to be; decide what kind of life you really want to live—with or without God.

I once had a meeting with two wonderful ladies in our local school association. Somehow in the course of our conversation, it got to the point where one of the ladies said she was an atheist. The other one said, "Oh, me too." They were saying that they do not believe in God, nor do they believe that God exists. I had already met several other people who felt the same way, so it came as no surprise to me. When I asked what made them think they are atheists, their answers focused on disbelief of all kinds of churches and religious practices around and on what they feel are hypocrisies. As a result they do not go to church. Since they do not go to church, they said they are then atheists.

Their objections are quite valid and natural. Why are there so many religions and denominations, so many beliefs and practices? That is not even the issue. How come even supposedly religious people cannot get along? How would you answer that? I did not offer an opinion. I simply listened then asked, "Have you ever had a moment when something was wrong, maybe an emergency or crisis in the family, that you remembered calling on God for help?" A moment of silence, then they were both honest to say, "Yes, that's true."

It is made clear that attending a church or even being a religious person or doing all kinds of charitable service does not make a person right with God. We cannot buy His favor. Do you think that when it is my turn to face God, he will actually ask me, "What is your religion," or "Which church do you go to?" I don't think so. Even before I approach our loving God, He already knows what's in my heart. That's His only basis. (We have no use of lawyers when it comes to Him.) All of us should be thankful that our merciful God is fair and just to look right into our hearts and spirit or soul and not our color, religion, or church affiliation, not even at our accomplishments or level of education. God's love has no discrimination.

God does not classify people according to religion or religious beliefs. He looks at us *individually* and knows if we are abiding or connected to Him or not. We are the *apple of His eyes,* and He will not withhold anything good from us. Sometimes He has to allow things to happen because we have an important lesson to learn in life or a purpose to accomplish. But if you keep *trusting* and *obeying* Him, everything will be all right at the end.

Judging others is not our job. That is His job. There are appointed judges on earth, yes, but ultimately He is the Judge of all. Our job is simple, to trust and obey Him, and love others whom He loves as well. Spread His love to everyone and notice how our environment, our world will be a better place to live.

Five Steps to Spiritual Health:

1. *Know that God is real.* (Because He is!) – Know that there is a God who truly cares about you, not only spiritually but as a whole being.

2. *Admit that you need God in your life.* – All you need is to believe in Him and that He is the only one who can answer all your questions and fill your every longing and need.

3. *Receive His free gift of love to you.*– All you need is to open your heart to Him, accept Him into your life, submit to His perfect plan for you and enjoy the experience of having a personal relationship with Him. It is an amazing healthy experience to discover the wonders of His love and grace.

4. *Get to know God better* – The more you know about Him and how special you really are to Him, the more you can enjoy your fellowship with Him.

If you are serious in your desire to know more about God, answer any questions you may have about Him; clear some doubts if there are any. I only know one authorized and reliable book that I can recommend: The Bible or, personally I call, the Book of Life. It is also the number one recommended reading by many highly successful, respected, and happy individuals who've found God as their true treasure. If you admire or acknowledge the wisdom and passion of great people like Abraham Lincoln, Martin Luther King Jr., Billy Graham, Mother Teresa, and so many other wise and accomplished people, it is this book that they acknowledged as their source of true knowledge and understanding.

The Book of Life has been the bestseller of all time since 1611. It is the only book translated into hundreds of languages and **dialects** and distributed to every corner of the world. It is being read and **treasured** by people of all walks of life, rich and poor, scholars, professo**rs, engine**ers, scientists, the famous, and simple everyday people.

This book is truly amazing. It is a complete library **by itself** and covers all subjects you could ever think of: love, marriage, **divorce**, child-rearing, family, law, medicine, business management, succ**ess, finance,** debt, taxes, history, math, etc., including our past, present, **and** future, and especially LIFE and how to live it. It was relevant and applicable four centuries ago and still is today.

By the way, I find it interesting that the very first schools, which did not have the supplies of books we have now, used this book as their textbook. If you can only read one book in your lifetime, this is it. It is worth every minute you spend reading it. You will get to know God better and find the answers to your questions. In it you will find life, your life, as well.

5. *Walk with Him daily* – In His Word He says, "I will never leave you nor forsake you." Believe it! He is there for you twenty-four hours a day, seven days a week, rain or shine, when you are awake or asleep. (If someone tells you otherwise, ask if that someone can do the same for you.) Our true God is faithful, and you can always count on Him. You will no longer feel so alone, lonely, or helpless anymore. You will find worrying as an obsolete subject. That surely will make you happy, and that is healthy!

Have you *filled in* the *blank* yet?

Is there really God's plan for each and all of us?

Before a book is written, the author already knows what he wants to achieve or accomplish at the end. Before the movie is done, the producer already has a story, a script. Same with our life; there may be some flexibility, the players may have their input or even decide to get off the line, but at the end the author or director decides the ending.

Mankind can always create manmade laws and opinions, but in the end only God's laws and principles prevail. You see, man has the free will, choice, or liberty to come up with whatever he or she wants to do or go to. However, there is a master designer who already designed a *master plan* for our best life to live…and incidentally, the universe is designed, or created, to follow that plan. That means man can always choose to say, "This is my way," but you probably already know what happens to those who choose their own way. When a person abides in or aligns with God, this choice determines whether the person is in tune or in harmony with the universe at the same time.

Let's take an illustration. Say God already prepared Highway 101 for us to take, and it leads to "Life of Abundance State." You want to get there, of course. You made your decision that Highway 101 is the best way for you to follow. You prepared the things you need for your trip adventure. You may still experience some bumps and challenges along the road; otherwise it is a smooth drive, singing along the way as you joyride. You are in constant peace, assured that you know exactly where you are going, and life is wonderful there!

In contrast, you have friends (Whoever, Whatever, Whenever) who somewhat also wish to go to "Life of Abundance State" (sure, everybody wants to go there!), but they have no particular plan or decision. They feel they are smarter and will take their own route or drive wherever, as long as they get there. But along with this chosen path come obstacles, distractions, loss of direction. Will they ever get to the original desired destination? We hope they could, if they find their way back to Highway 101, the only way, but they probably won't.

You see, in a way we are all like the famous story, apparently told around the world in variations, about the *Prodigal Son*. He has a loving father who is very wealthy. This son decided to get his inheritance early and left to live his life his own way. He splurged and had lots of fun, until he lost everything he had and was forced to live the life of a beggar and an outcast, a life of misery. Then he remembered his father, how great his life could have been if he were with him. He found his way back HOME and found his father, who spotted him from afar because he had been waiting for him. The father joyfully welcomed him, gave him a big hug, and prepared a big feast for his coming home…and as he found himself again, where he truly belonged, he began to live abundantly ever after.

Thoughts to ponder/something to think about:
Natural vs. manmade could affect wellness.

I am not saying that manmade is wrong, because we have plenty of great, wonderful, beneficial manmade creations such as light bulbs, computers, resorts, etc. But on a few manmade things, take caution, because they could be harmful to your health and sometimes can lead to destruction. Some examples include:

Processed Food – The more fresh and natural the food that you eat, the more nutrients or vitamins you get, and the better it is for your health. An example is eating raw or steamed vegetables instead of canned. Most processed food and drinks may look attractive or have great flavor, but they are stripped or void of necessary nutrients we need to maintain good health. Great examples are refined white sugar, table salt, bleached flours, sodas, candies and cakes. Try to stay away from refined, processed, bleached, engineered, etc., which a few food experts refer to as poisons to the extreme. These can help fill you up but could be doing you more harm than good overall, over time. Now, do not play a guilt trip if you take a little, because if it helps someone eat, a little is better than not being able to eat at all. All I am bringing is consciousness to take caution or take those in moderation, until gradually you can reduce using these to the point that you can begin to appreciate that natural foods also have taste, and they are better. To attest to this, after reading this section, my dear friend commented, "This is true! I started doing this slowly, and after a few months, I was finally craving healthy food instead of junk food. I feel so much better now. I buy fresh produce and organic occasionally. I even make it to the 'health food' grocery store now and then. I never thought I could *not* eat sugar and lots of processed food, but I *can*! And I feel great! It just took some discipline and a comparably short amount of time." I laughed with joy as I felt her excitement.

Advice and Opinion – I do listen to and respect people's advice and opinions, then I put those into consideration. I verify if what I gathered is right or wrong based on my own research study, own experience, and pure common sense before I draw my own conclusion and/or make a decision. People are entitled to their opinions, but that does not make their opinions mine, nor does it make mine yours and theirs. We are all different and unique, and so are our situations. Advice and opinions are manmade. Experience and common sense are more natural than manmade. Personally I try to stay away from people's opinions or advice. I learned if at all possible not to give advice or opinions. When asked or pressed to give one, I offer people information or resources instead. An effort to *be informed*, coupled with pure common sense, tends to produce better results. So, next time people offer you advice or opinions, if you trust them enough, that may be easier to take; for the rest, it is always best to verify first and make up your own mind. And I hope you'll do that with the information I am providing in this book to guide you when you are to make your own decision. This way you can always take the full responsibility for your decisions and actions. Blaming somebody else for the advice or opinion they gave does not work.

Religion – Let us be clear about this: religion is not the same as spirituality, as being religious does not necessarily mean you are spiritually healthy. Religion is the *gathering of people* of the same belief or cause. Being so many types, they are being referred to as various religious organizations. Spirituality, on the other hand, pertains to all and anyone's need or longing for a close or meaningful *relationship with God*, who is acknowledged as the source and creator of life Himself and who unconditionally loves each of us. Religion tends to separate people. Only God's love brings people together. I have considered this subject for a long time because of its sensitivity. But at this point I am more comfortable than ever to say that the sensitivity of the subject is because religion is nothing but manmade and somehow always manages to create controversy, arguments, conflicts, separations, and to the extreme, wars. I stand to what I declared a few years back, "Religion tends to separate people. Only God's love brings people together." Humans, because of uniqueness and differences, have naturally created many types of religions, churches, synagogues, organizations, etc., all over the planet, but failed to bring the true *peace* and *love,* which we all desire in this universe. Nowhere in the Book of Life do I see religion or being religious encouraged. The churches are there, and they are good and encouraged, but these are being referred to as gathering or fellowship of believers, not mere buildings. Furthermore, the Book of Life is very clear as repeatedly stating that the Spirit of God does not dwell in buildings or temples made with hands, but He dwells *in* those who believe and receive Him. That is how He can be with us wherever we are, not only when we are inside a church, synagogue, or temple. So, who will/can I believe best to rule my life? The religions that created so many rules and doctrines which alienate me from the other people whom God also loves, or the one and only living God who dwells in me, whose only two rules are: first, *love God with all your being*, and second, *love others as you love your self?* I believe you can see that the answer to this question is simple.

Different religions believe in or have their own prophet, but as far as I have studied, prophets are not God, and true prophets teach true love and peace to everyone and acknowledge that there is someone bigger and better than them that they, too, refer to as their God or Most High. These thousands of religious practices, the true Living God worshipping ones at least (not those that simply brought up their own hidden self-serving agendas), seem to agree on one thing, that in spite of all these differences in religious beliefs or practices, there is only *one true God*, also referred to as *Teacher, Protector, Savior, Provider, Redeemer, Master Healer*, and more. If we can all just learn to focus on this *one Most High, the one and only true Living God, the Ultimate Divine Power, the Almighty One*, whom we believe and worship, then we can possibly cause and bring more peace, love, and healing in all our lands. So next time, it may help to simply stay away from conversation with somebody else about these manmade religions, but embrace everyone just for the fact that God loves us all.

Talking about this subject reminds me of a portion in the Book of Life that may be familiar to you, as it is popularly read on many occasions. It is usually referred to as the *Love* Chapter, 1 Corinthians 13:

Though I speak with the tongues of men and of angels, but have not love, I have become sounding brass or a clanging cymbal.

And though I have the gift of prophecy and understand all mysteries and all knowledge, and though I have all faith, so that I could remove mountains, but have not love, I am nothing. And though I bestow all my goods to feed the poor, and though I give my body to be burned, but have not love, it profits me nothing.

Love endures and is kind; love does not envy; love does not parade itself, is not arrogant; does not behave rudely, does not seek its own, is not provoked, thinks no evil; does not rejoice in iniquity, but rejoices in the truth; bears all things, believes all things, hopes all things, endures all things. Love never fails…

When I was a child, I spoke as a child, I understood as a child, I thought as a child; but when I became a man, I put away childish things. For now we see in a mirror, dimly, but then face to face. Now I know in part, but then I shall know just as I also am known. And now abide faith, hope, love, these three; but the greatest of these is *love*.

> "A piece of the miracle process has been reserved for each of us."
>
> Jim Rohn, entrepreneur,
> author, speaker

Social Health

To be socially healthy is not difficult at all when you feel good, have the right attitude, have respect and consideration for others, etc. There is no need to struggle with trying to please everybody. You can never please everybody. Just be yourself; it will come. The more you understand yourself, the more you will understand others and better relate with them. Furthermore, to be socially adaptive and happy, remember that:

1. *We are all unique individuals* – We are all different from one another. As previously discussed, no two individuals in this world are exactly alike in appearance, way of thinking, mood or feelings, lifestyle, likes and dislikes, beliefs and opinions, etc. Not even identical twins born and raised together are exactly alike. Each of us is special. So do not expect others to think the same way you do, and don't be irritated if others do it differently or have different opinions. Learn to respect others' individualities so they respect yours as well.

2. *We are all created equal* – At first you may disagree. You may say, "How come there are those who are rich and those who are poor? Some are short, some are tall; some are pretty, some are not very pretty; some are black, brown, white, etc." Yes, that is true. That is all part of us being different and unique individuals. But in many ways we are the same and are created equal, and no one should feel left out or disadvantaged. Each of us has the opportunity to excel, to be the best that we can be in spite of our imperfections. Opportunities may vary but are equally available for all of us.

Somehow we become more focused on how we are different, forgetting how we are all also the same. We all have the same basic needs. None of us can live without food, water, and oxygen. We are balanced and equal in a way that no matter what your sex is, color, education, or socioeconomic background, each person has a problem or some imperfection in his or her life. This includes royalty and the rich and famous, who supposedly have everything! Maybe some of them even envy an ordinary person's freedom and privacy. Having so much wealth can actually become a burden or a big challenge to many of them. They cannot go around freely because they are always concerned about their safety. So which life do you want to have? Amazingly you will always find two people on each end of the rope wanting to switch ends with each other.

3. *We all affect one another* – Positively or negatively, whether we like it or not, we do. Be angry or happy and watch how the people around you react. It is highly contagious! So, spread more good tidings to our environment. Be happy. Be positive!

4. *Put yourself in someone's shoes* – You've probably heard the Golden Rule to treat others as you want to be treated. How would you feel, think, react if you were in their position. Understand instead of criticizing or judging. Don't be so quick to take things personally when a person around you seems to be angry with you or ignores you. It is possible that the person has a personal problem that is affecting him that may have nothing to do with you at all.

5. *Do not take your loved ones for granted* – Life is too short. Express your love in words and in deeds while you can. Spending time with your loved ones is the best expression of love and care you can give. Don't wait to do a good deed tomorrow. Do it now.

6. *Life is a give and take process* – The more you learn to be a giver, the more will come back to you. Give your love, your time, talent, or whatever else you can share. It is your best investment. You cannot lose, and you will be happy with its return. Learn to be a gracious receiver also, for you will then have more to give.

Financial Health

The following is an overview of the most challenging financial issues we currently face as individuals and as a society. These challenges affect all of us and call for everyone to seek and contribute for immediate solutions.

Are you ready to retire? If you are a senior or approaching retirement, then you are most likely already aware of the problem the baby boomers are facing right now. Are you aware of the report below released by the US Department of Labor? I first learned of it in the 1980s. Over twenty years ago it was like this, and it is not getting any better but worse. I am just amazed how many seniors are neither aware of nor prepared for this impending predicament.

According to the US Department of Labor, of every one hundred people who reach age sixty-five, only 2 are financially independent, 23 must continue working, and 75 must depend on friends, charity, or relatives. Of every one hundred Americans reaching age sixty-five today, a horrifying 96 are *flat broke*.

I thought things would get better, but not only that, the retirement age is delayed to sixty-seven, and I am seeing the reality with more seniors continuously working to supplement their income. Will you be financially secure, dependent on others, or will you continue to work through supposed retirement age?

In an October 2005 issue of *TIME Magazine*, a front page headline reads, *"The Great Retirement Rip Off – Millions of Americans who think they will retire with benefits are in for a nasty surprise… TIME magazine investigates why the Golden Years are in peril."* The article features pictures of seniors, one collecting cans and another still working at age seventy-eight, working just to supplement their income and pay their medical bills.

Now, the latest concern that should sound an alarm for everyone in America, regardless of age, is best expressed by Donald Trump and Robert Kiyosaki in the book they coauthored, aptly titled *Why We Want You To Be Rich*: "We are losing our middle class, and a shrinking middle class is a threat to the stability of America and to the world democracy itself… The financial problems we all face are now bigger than the U.S. government alone can handle…" (pages 1 and 75).

Can the course of the financial crisis taking place in America, and in some respects around the globe, be changed?

Findings show that the segment of our population that does not make enough money to meet their basic needs is growing alarmingly. That is true, but at the same time there are just too many people depending on our government to supply for their basic existence or supplement their income so that they may live and pay for their medical needs. Those with disabilities, who are truly unable to work, and our seniors, who fairly made their contributions, are well justified in expecting the government to fulfill its promises. More alarming is our population's younger generation who has joined the generations of dependents in our society called the *welfare system*. This is becoming a huge burden because the individuals are not able to function as healthy and productive members of our society. Is it possible to affect a change on people's dependent tendencies?

Financial matters and money have always been a major part of our everyday lives. Some do it well, and some do not. Nobody likes to be financially unstable, but it can happen to anybody. I have found out that financial education is very important to young children as soon as they start to receive money and begin learning how to spend it. The following tips, as a start, could contribute to an individual's financial health.

It takes self-discipline not to spend what you do not have. It is wiser to wait a little bit to save the money you need to buy what you need instead of charging it now and then suffering a long time, realizing you are paying about twice as much due to the interest. By my own experience, I learned the hard way that using credit for purchases instead of ready cash only benefited the lenders. It was too late for me and many to realize that we only infused financial trouble to ourselves. At the end, people suffer financially; and the lenders feel it as well.

No matter how good the advertising, stay away from using credit cards! Experience should teach you that the plastics should be used only for their original purpose, identification and emergency use. Discard the word convenient, for it is certainly not.

When you pay by cash, it helps control your spending since you cannot buy what you do not have the money for. At least you will go home with no headache or worry about paying for it later. It is so easy to charge everything that it can get out of hand. The result, in most cases, is very ugly. People who faced collection, repossession, bankruptcy, or foreclosure experienced tremendous amount of stress, pain, humiliation, etc. Some experienced mental and emotional trauma beyond what they felt they could handle, which caused unnecessary cases of divorce, suicide, and violent crime. The realization that *you don't really own anything if a portion is still owed from others*, regardless of how much you've invested on it, is beginning to sink into people's minds. The foreclosure tsunami, credit crisis, and the long-term recession of the late 2000s will never be easily forgotten. A lot of lessons will be learned by individuals and various sectors of our society from these related experiences. I for one learned a lot and will carry and share these lessons to many for as long as I live. I am seeing the reality of this phrase I heard before, "The borrowers become slaves to the lenders."

Have you heard of the other AIDS that is deadlier than the actual disease itself? This one has already affected close to ninety percent of our nation's population. The *acquired income deficiency syndrome* has been sweeping the nation at a very alarming rate. Wake up! Know what we are dealing with here. The first thing you can do if you are affected is to *learn to live within your means*. Before buying anything, try to answer these questions first:

1. Do I need it?

2. Can I afford it? Or can it wait?

3. Is it tax deductible?

4. Is it good for me long-term? Will it grow?

If you honestly answer *yes* to at least three of these questions, then you cannot go wrong. If not, or you have any doubts, take the necessary caution. Am I making an issue about buying? I guess I am, because this is when we stumble the most, don't we? Yes, we want to help move our economy by spending, but when people now suffer because of spending by credit or with money that they don't have in the first place (even our government does this), our society will suffer at the end. People need to wake up to the reality that our special, memorable holidays have become too commercialized. Have you not notice yet that we just have too many occasions to celebrate now? Do we really have to be in debt just for decor and costumes? Isn't this all about *business* and merchants making money? Do we really still experience the true meaning of the occasions when we are financially burdened? Isn't just being with the people we love or care about, just having simple dinner get-togethers, more than sufficient? Continuing with the trap of financial bondage, or starting fresh focusing more on the meaning and value of our actions and expenditures, of course, remains to be a matter of choice.

Learn to *budget*. It is simpler than you think. I have to admit that I really did not learn about this until age twenty-two when I started receiving a paycheck or what I could call real income. Prior to that, I really did not have any money to budget. I sometimes wonder if they even taught budgeting in school. Nevertheless, I started to learn, which was fun at first especially when I had more income than expenses. Then I got married and had three children. Life got more complicated. I then began to learn more about negative balance, deficit, and the need for a strict budget.

Let me share with you some techniques I learned from the experts coupled with my own experiences. As a starter, regardless of your age or financial situation, you can do simple budgeting:

First, get a notebook. Draw a vertical line down the middle (or fold it in half). Next, write on the left "Income," or what is coming in on a monthly basis from all resources. If it varies, figure out the most reasonable average amount or use the lowest figure to be safe. Then write "Expenses" on the right. Below that, write down all your expenses, including but not limited to: basic necessities, according to priorities like house payment, food/grocery, insurances, utilities, car payment and gas, etc. Write down the actual or most realistic figures you can; check your receipts, checkbook, charge account, etc. Evaluate and differentiate the needs/necessities vs. extras/wants. Note that your expenses should not exceed your income. They should either balance, or ideally, your income should always exceed your expenses (even a little) so you have something to set aside for *savings* (planned vacations, things to buy, family reunions, etc.), for an *emergency fund* (important for any unforeseen needs like auto repairs, medical problems, lay-offs, etc., and for *investments* (retirement, children's college, etc.). At least three months' emergency income is recommended by the experts and more if possible. *Planning* is very important. Small, gradual savings or investments are definitely much better than nothing. *Insurance* is very important, especially life and health. The least understood one I have seen is life insurance. Either people have been throwing away so much money on their insurance, are underinsured, or have no protection at all. It is alarming that many families are left financially devastated when the breadwinners pass away without any form of life insurance to protect them. When the insurance premium cost could be as little or even lesser than car insurance. We are required to protect our cars through car insurance. Shouldn't we be protecting our families more?

If your expenses are higher, be alarmed. That is a warning sign that you are not financially well. Unlike a fever, this one does not go away by itself. You have to do something to get back on track, or you will be in more trouble later. Evaluate your expenses and see which ones you can cut or eliminate. You may wish to stick more with water for a while than colored drinks; after all, plain water is healthier. Do you really have to have so many channels on your television? Do you even have time to watch all the channels? A better question is, how much productive time do you (and the children) spend or waste in front of the tube? Do you have to shop for more clothes that most likely will just crowd your closet or buy more things that just stock up in the garage? I was twice guilty of this, that's how I know. Keep finding alternatives, ways and means to save. Some people are wiser financially and are getting ahead, more secure and worry free, while a lot of us are more naïve and have to learn the hard way. We hope that our future generations will be wiser.

When you have a balanced budget, you do not have to worry about the pressure of having another job. You would not need anything beyond your eight hours of work to still enjoy your life. You did not come into this world just to work twelve to sixteen hours or more a day just to pay your bills or worry about your bills, did you? Your *budget sheet* is one of your most important assignments for life, so keep up with it.

The following is an example of a very basic monthly budget sheet.

My Financial Picture (Simple Budget Example)

Income (per month)	**Expenses** (per month)
Take home pay: $3,500.	Giving (you decide): $400.
	Savings/Emergency: $400.
	Residence: $1,000.
	Auto Expenses: $500.
Other Sources: $ 500.	Insurances: $200.
	Groceries: $800.
	Utilities: $250.
	Credits: $250.
	Misc.: $200.
TOTAL: $4,000.	TOTAL: $4,000.

Note: This is only an example. The actual one you will create will be based on your situation. This is to bring realization of your current financial picture so you can be more aware of the areas to improve.

Remember this saying, "It is not how much money you make that counts; it is what you keep!" The savings and emergency section under *expenses* are for the saying, "Pay yourself first (if you can)!" There are many books available that you can read to help you further on this subject as there is actually a lot more to learn; for example, *assets* minus *liabilities* can determine your *net worth*. Want to see yours? It's simple: total assets (worth of what you own) minus total liabilities (what you owe) equals your net worth. How is yours?

Establishing your *long-term* and *short-term goals* is helpful.

Example:

Long-term goals: To establish financial stability within two to five years. (This may vary.)

Short-term goals are designed to establish your *plan of action* to reach your goal/dream. These specific execution plans will help you toward the achievement of your long-term goals. This can be done on a daily, weekly, or monthly basis, whichever is applicable. These may include: making your decision to give your best at your current income resource; evaluating your ideas/dreams, true interests, talents and abilities for career consideration where you can be most successful long-term; incorporate personal development and more training toward your established goals; public relations or networking with others who can be helpful to you personally and your career, etc.

Other important things to consider:
- *Live within your means.* Stay out of debt as much as possible, as soon as possible. Develop the discipline to maintain only one to two credit cards for the purpose of identification and extreme emergency only. You probably have already heard that there are two types of debt: good credit and bad credit. Learn the difference. Learn to use the good one, and stay away from the bad one that can enslave you and keep you in poverty.
- *Set your priorities, always remembering the giving principle.* Set aside at least the first ten percent to cheerfully give as your seed, to your church and/or other worthy causes you believe in. Remember, it is when you give that you receive.
- *Pay yourself before all the bills.* Save or invest on a systematic, periodic deductions like a 401K or IRA plan, provided the plan still makes sense for the current economic condition. Otherwise, consider converting your existing plan to a "self-directed IRA." (Yes, it can be done!) You may also want to consider the possibility of investing on affordable lands, preferably close to metros or developments. Learn yourself or consult someone you can trust about *land banking* and *self-directed retirement plans* to help you on these areas before making a move. Always consider and update your *emergency funds*, *retirement plans*, and *insurances* (life, health, long-term care or retirement, auto—in that order).

Learning to manage what you have is the trick of the financial game. Many of those who have won the lotto, received an inheritance, made millions on movies, in sports, in business, etc., lost when they spent their money carelessly or trusted the wrong person to handle their finances. A lot of them ended up broke. It is equally interesting that there are people who have learned to live a simple, worry-free life, feeling rich and secure, even with little income, just because they know how to manage what they have wisely…and that is healthy.

> *"What can be added to the happiness of a man who is in health, out of debt, and has a clear conscience?"*
>
> Adam Smith, economist
> and philosopher

Health Balance and Priorities

Now that you are more familiar with the six vital areas of your being and how to meet each need, we can discuss how these areas can work together harmoniously as *one healthy total being*.

First, we need to know *balance*. That means each part of our being is equally important and must always be considered; each needs to be evenly met. Not one can be disregarded or ignored otherwise there will be an imbalance, which is not healthy at all. Result: an unhealthy, unfulfilled individual. Similar to a balanced diet, each basic food group is important and has to be supplied to maintain good health. When a person only takes bread and water all day long for months, his diet is unbalanced and his dietary needs are not fully met. He may get by for a few days but will eventually be malnourished and become sick. We do not want that to happen. We can prevent this unnecessary waste of valuable resources.

These inseparable, integrated parts are assembled according to some medically related schools (like a team) and presented as follows:

Physical-Mental-Emotional-Spiritual-Social

(Financial not normally included).

To have a winning team, each player has to be healthy, always present, and prepared to *play and win with the team*. In a team no individual is more important than the others, and no one can be disregarded. Each cannot be doing his own thing. A team is just not designed that way. Each player is aware of the different members' functions on the team. It is the team's goal to be able to learn to *work together* as *one* to be a winning team. When that goal is accomplished, a great, beautiful performance and result can be expected as the play of a real WINNING TEAM.

Just like on any team though, *leadership* is equally important. That is why we have a head coach to direct the team, a quarterback to execute a football play, and a team leader to coordinate and make sure that the job gets done. Can you imagine a team with players just doing their own thing? It is not possible for each and every member to assume the leadership role. Anyone can try, but will find out later that it does not work. It will be chaos, and eventually the team could lose the game. One person, the most qualified one, has to take the leadership. This is where *priority*, or proper line up, comes.

To build a winning team, it is important to consider who will take the lead. This point is very crucial. It is vital to be able to choose the *right one* to take the lead in order to have a better chance of winning. "We cannot afford so many mistakes. We cannot afford to lose." These are the statements that have been the game's guiding principle. One has to be chosen for the leading role. "We are here (to play) to win!" That is the *goal*. Could we not say and apply the same thing to our game of *life*? If careful consideration is not made with no particular goal or purpose, each of our parts will tend to do their own thing, uncoordinated and disorganized. The end result in a person will be confusion, frustration, and in the worse cases, even mental or emotional breakdown.

Here is the mystery of life disclosed for you and me. It is nothing new. It has been available for ages and for generations but remains undisclosed and undiscovered by many. Those happy and victorious people I have talked about; they each declared the following *life's guiding principles* as their main source or key for a happy, healthy, successful, victorious life. For years I have searched. Through my own personal experiences, I have tested their validity. Check them out and judge for yourself:

Can *physical* effectively take the lead? We already know the answer to that. How about mental and emotional? *Mental* is more apt to directions and programming or conditioning. *Emotional* is reactive, and can you really imagine being led by your emotions? It will not work. How about social or financial? Can you really allow the people or things surrounding you to direct your life? It is just not appropriate.

So, we are left with *spiritual*, the most left-out, disregarded, and avoided one. Why are we humans so stubborn and blind to see that in the first place? Because we have been blindfolded, lied to, and too distracted to recognize the truth and see clearly what is really good for us. This is our chance to now unveil and expose the *truth* of what our *spiritual* side, submitted to and having a personal relationship with God, can do. As the right spirit becomes the driving force of your whole being, it is amazing that there is a definite command to the brain to embrace the good things and delete or reject the bad input. This can take time, but each day is a progress. When your inputs are good and positive, the actions and outcomes are good and positive as well. No longer will the impulsive physical be the driving force, but the responsible and conscientious *spirit* will now direct the mind and the other parts of your being. Here is the *Secret of Total Wellness and Success in Life* formula:

Spirit → Mind → Emotion → Body → Relationship → Finance
Life is not all about money or making money.

When you are mentally right, this can easily cause your emotions to act rightly as well. The spirit, mind, and emotion can then automatically direct the physical body to behave and take care of itself better, the social to relate or build better relationship with others, and direct the financial to manage its spending money and resources wisely. If you are on this track, will you be better off socially? Relating and dealing with people somehow becomes no problem when you think and feel good, are considerate of others, and are doing your best to live your life in good harmony with yourself and others. It becomes automatic. This I believe is very much consistent with what I read in the Book of Life, *Seek God first and all things shall be added to you.* (See Book of Life Reference List)

> *"You can be anything you want to be, if you only believe with sufficient conviction and act in accordance with your faith; for whatever the mind can conceive and believe, it can achieve."*
>
> Napoleon Hill

Understanding the Secrets of Life

Could it be that people are lost or suffer because of lack of knowledge?

Life is wonderful! Life is colorful, truly beautiful…if you can relate to what I am talking about. A lot of people don't see it that way. They are still wrapped up with the life complexities and challenges, and without much understanding of the nature of what they are dealing with or how to go about these challenges, life surely can bog one down.

Realize that life is not a bed of roses, as the saying goes. Come to think of it, as beautiful as the roses are, people sometimes forget that this favorite flower comes with thorns that can hurt if you are not careful or have not learned how to deal with them. Life can be better understood.

- Life is *a process*. We can better appreciate our life in comparison to precious gems or metals like diamonds or gold, which need to go through the refining process to get to their best form for best value and appreciation.
- Life is like *a wheel*. Sometimes you are *up*, sometimes you are *down*. It is a way of life that makes it more beautiful or colorful, once you understand the principle. How can you go anywhere if the wheel on your vehicle is not moving up and down? Can you imagine your life with the same food, tasks, etc. Life will be monotonous; people get bored. That's why change is a must and a welcome word to those who understand. The stock market, the making and losing of money, does not exist without the wheel principle. Imagine a person at the intensive care unit with the heart monitor showing a straight line instead of the up and down flow. This principle is important to keep us and our economy alive and well. So, don't get too scared when things are down (temporarily), because the good news is, when you reach the bottom, the only other way is *up*!
- Life has its *seasons*. Yes, everything around us helps us understand life. You can compare life to the seasons that we

have to go through, whether we like them or not. *Autumn* is when our days begin to be gloomy; then comes the challenging cold *winter*; then the beautiful *spring* comes like a fresh new beginning, full of colors and fresh new leaves on once seemingly dead or bare trees; then comes *summer* full of sunshine, when people comes out to enjoy the sun! Regardless of the season, if you understand and see what are the best things you can get or do out of every situation, every season or situation has something good to offer. This is the reason why people go out and enjoy the snow during winter instead of just hibernating at home. Same with a true real estate investor who is having a ball purchasing his investment properties while the rest are feeling gloomy about the real estate market. It is how you *make the best out of every situation* that you can come out *winning in life*.

To follow are some of detailed explanations that can help bring some light to our search for *life*.

The Way of Life

This section hopes to give you some understanding on *why we were who we were, and why we are who we are now*. It will also give some insights as to what you and I can still be. Interestingly, the more you understand yourself, the more you will understand OTHERS also and what goes around us in relation to each other on a daily basis. My main basis for this topic is what I learned from my nursing school regarding *human growth and development process,* together with life's actual experiences and observation, which verify or validate the given information.

Have you ever seen a newborn baby that looks devilish? I don't think so. At least I haven't. They all look so cute—sweet little angels, so adorable, so harmless and cuddly. But what happens after some years? How come some grow up to be so different?

You see, as a child is born and begins to grow and develop, he is like a dry sponge that hungrily and willingly absorbs everything that is given or presented to him. Besides his natural genes from his parents, everything that he takes in affects his growth and development. The food that he eats, his environment, including everything that he sees, hears, feels, and the significant people who provide for him, will register in his mental and emotional processes. The adequacy or lack of stimulation and of meeting his basic needs physically, mentally, emotionally, spiritually, and socially will greatly determine how well the child will adapt in life.

Children are called mimics or "copycats" because that's how they learn. They *copy*! They exhibit and express what they were in a sense programmed to do. The *first three years*, considered the most critical stage of one's life, are all absorption. So do not think that babies and toddlers are unaware. They are. That is why it is very important to be careful of what we expose them to. This is also the reason why toddlers question a lot. (Development ages, by the way, vary for each individual; some develop earlier, some later.) Lots of *love* to develop the sense or feeling of *security* at this early stage is very important. At *four to seven years*, children are still very responsive to cueing, directions, instructions, and guidance. This is the best time to teach vital information, to reinforce values. So let us not be too hard on our children; they are but a mirror or reflection of their environment.

What you may also find interesting is that each child from birth exhibits natural or innate abilities to adapt, to learn, and to develop. Isn't it fascinating to watch an infant open his mouth and turn his head toward his mother's nipple when he is hungry, even with his eyes closed? Then watch that incredible sucking reflex begin to work. Mind you, no one has to teach him that. Thank God, because even a genius or a pediatric expert would have a hard time teaching a baby such an important survival step. Another is the natural instinct to blink when a foreign object approaches or gets in the eye, causing tears to naturally flow to try to wash it out. There is the coughing reflex, or the body's cells' ability to reproduce, etc. These are just a few of *the wonders of our being*. Of course, we have the scientific and medical explanations, but still, where do all these marvelous abilities come from? We have these *natural abilities* since childhood, naturally *built in*. It could not just disappear, right? Did we forget, or did we allow somebody to steal or distract us?

By the time the child is *eight to thirteen* years old, he tends to become more selective of what to willingly take or what to reject as he begins to develop independence. This is good and should be encouraged with proper care and guidance.

During teenage years, when the child is *thirteen to nineteen* years old, he no longer accepts being called a child. He would rather be recognized as a *young adult* or, more appropriately, a *teen*. At this time it is natural for him to think that he already knows everything. (The best way to understand our children at this stage is simply to recall how we were at that time.) After all, his sponge is pretty much filled up with things he has seen, heard, and felt. He figures he has everything he needs to be able to be on *his own*. This is the time the teen needs to learn that, along with the independence he is beginning to claim, there comes a great deal of *responsibility*. When he was a young child, he was very much dependent on his parents and other adults around him. The parents and those adults *were responsible* for him. But as the child grows and declares independence, he has to learn and begin to accept responsibility and *accountability* for his own decisions and actions. With the independence the teen still needs continuous guidance in making choices and decisions. When he becomes an adult, or as soon as he assumes full independence, he will carry those lessons along with him. If we adults fail to teach our children *responsibility* and *accountability*, it is chaos. Pointing fingers, blaming others does not work.

From the *early teens to about twenty five*, life is an interesting adventure, a true learning process. After experimenting with and testing what the individual knows or thinks he knows, the young learner now begins to sort, to validate, and to evaluate if the information he got is actually good or bad for him. Those who have received good nurturing or good programming early in life can adjust to society better and faster with feelings of security and confidence. Those who did not will have more difficulty adjusting because there is still so much to sort out. Confusion, anger, rebellion, or regression may be demonstrated. A feeling of insecurity and lack of confidence or trust in oneself or others may be experienced, making it a very difficult time for those who are in this situation. Violent crimes, movies, TV shows, videogames, magazines, and other forms of media expose our children to more unwanted predicaments. Come to think of it, it is becoming a concern for what type of world we are molding now. A high divorce rate, conflicts, and violence even among family members are a reflection of the effect of previous "programming".

Two situations may arise in this particular case. First, the dangerous side is for those who simply say, "I give up. This is what I am, and this is what I will be." The second, on a more positive side, may say, "This may be my situation now, but I can make it different. I am not a hopeless case." We have already heard a lot of people who were branded as "born on the wrong side of town" or who have "no hope or future." But these great men and women stood up, fought, persevered, made a huge difference in their lives, and eventually shared the same opportunity and success as others.

Things can change. *People can change.* In fact, as much as we resist it, *change* is one thing that is always constant. Change for the better is always good! It is a matter of *decision,* what a person chooses to take, to do, to follow. This is what you call *reprogramming* or *reconditioning.* A person at any age between *twenty and forty* or even younger, as soon as he becomes fully aware of what or who he is, can assume responsibility for his life's direction. He can now decide what to take and keep or what to reject or delete from his program. He can reshape and reprogram his future to what it will be or what he can be. It can be done if the person chooses to, especially if a supportive environment is available.

"Life begins at forty," is a saying that seems to fit the assumption that, by that age, experiences should have taught us enough lessons to gain wisdom. We now have a better chance to live our lives the way they should be. Do our children really have to wait that long and go through the things we have been through before they learn important, basic life principles?

Learning is an endless process. Even college graduates have not yet finished their schooling, at least not in the real arena of life. Learning goes on as life goes on. Even our seniors can still learn. It is never too late for anyone. Each can still grow and develop more mature, learn new skills, and learn better ways to make life worth living. Yes, just be an *open* door for more and greater opportunities. After all, this is the way of life.

I can very well relate to this because in spite of my age and vast amount of information accumulated, I remain curious and eager to learn new things, what's going on. As a result, my life remains exciting with a new adventure each day, and I certainly continue to benefit from newfound information, resources, friends, and contacts. Continuous *learning* is exciting! It keeps me young and productive, verifying the *secrets* of those happy, vibrant seniors I interviewed in the past who shared, *"Just don't stop learning new things and be happy."*

In fact, learn to *relax*, learn to *sing* and *dance*, learn your best *smile*, *laugh* more often, learn to *live* with *passion*… Live to your fullest potential!

> *"Always be a first-rate version of yourself instead of a second-rate version of somebody else."*
>
> Judy Garland, singer

Life as a Puzzle

Life is like a *puzzle*. When you open the box and see the hundred or thousand pieces all jumbled together, it seems so hopelessly complicated that it is almost impossible to imagine putting it together. In fact, some will hesitate or refuse to even try right there. Just like this book, each section or chapter remains as a piece of the puzzle until you read its entirety. You can then visualize the total picture, that everything in it actually fits together. Sometimes life seems too complex and puzzling, but in the end it all makes sense. In that way, putting one's life together can be likened to putting a puzzle together. If you work at it, allow enough time and perseverance, it can be done. Once you are familiar with the pieces, it becomes a lot easier. To put the pieces of your puzzle of life together, you need to take the following steps:

- *Gain some knowledge.* Learn the basics of life. Learn how to sort out the pieces and how to put them together. Apply what you have learned.
- Learn to *organize* and *prioritize*. Let's take a typical puzzle picture of a barn in a field in spring all jumbled up in the box. You cannot just randomly pick out pieces and try to put them

together. It is harder and takes much longer to do it that way. First, put the colors together. The flowers and greens together, the reds or browns for the barn, the blues and whites for the sky. Remember, each piece and each group is important and actually represents something. These groups of colors represent the positives and the good things in life. Always focus on them first, then you will find it easier to put your puzzle of life together. The black or dark pieces that seem to show nothing; what about them? They are needed, too. Those are the dark periods of our life, trials included, which are somehow necessary to make the picture of our life complete. They will eventually accent the colors in our life. For how can we appreciate the brighter sides of life (love, joy, and peace) if we do not experience some dark sides (test, trials, sadness, loneliness)? It would be a dull, meaningless life.

- Learn to *persevere*. Life's challenges are so many and so often that it would be easy to quit before the fruits of our labor are realized. But if one perseveres and overcomes adversity, a wonderful outcome can be achieved.

When the puzzle picture is complete, like when a goal is achieved, you will find that it is not really impossible to put together a masterpiece. It is amazing to find that those separate pieces that looked so confusing now make sense and actually fit together. That apparently everything we go through in life, everything about us and around us, *fits*.

As you work on your personal puzzle of life, picture that barn in the field on a beautiful day in spring. Now, as you organize the pieces together according to color classification, you will also remember what each group represents in your life. Focus on these three:
1. The *barn* – your *storage of blessings*. What are they?
2. The *field* – your *gifts, special talents, and skills*. What are they?
3. The *blue sky* and *white clouds* – your *goals, dreams, and wishes*. What are they?

The *barn*, or your storage of blessings, is your storage of strength and source of security. Each of us has something to put on the list, so count all your blessings inside that barn, everything that you have that you are thankful for. Remind yourself of how blessed you really are. Even if you think you have nothing to be thankful for, the fact that you are alive is actually a blessing. That means God is not finished with you yet. Keep your hope, your faith that something good is about to happen, that something good is in store for you. Open the door and windows of your barn, look up to the sky, and ask for His blessings to pour upon you—not just money, but health, happiness, peace, and wisdom. If you truly believe, are willing to wait, and you continue to strive as He leads you, then you can expect God to deliver for you.

The *field* or garden with scattered flowers represents your God-given talents and special gifts that were uniquely designed and given to you. They also include the skills you have acquired. Like the plants and flowers, they need to be discovered, identified, and nurtured for one to fully enjoy their beauty and benefits. Don't be shy. Bring them out. Find out what you are good at, what you are interested in, and develop these talents and skills. You will find that these assets can help bring meaning to your life. Eventually you will be able to share your gifts with others and fulfill your life's purpose.

The *blue sky* and *white cloud* represent your goals, dreams, and wishes, which, like the sky, are endless. Have you heard of the phrase "The sky is the limit"? That means your realm of opportunity is actually endless and has no boundaries. Mistakes, failures, or even the most difficult trials should neither stop you nor slow you down. Arise and embrace the challenges of life. While you are still alive, there are a lot more doors for you to open, more options and opportunities for you to discover. Go on, pursue your dreams, your goals, your wishes. They are there for a purpose. Consider this phrase: *"Whatever your mind can conceive and believe, you can achieve" (Napoleon Hill)*. It is as simple as thinking about eating a delicious ice cream and then going to the freezer or store to make that happen. It is as possible as the man who dreamed of stepping on the moon. His impossible dream became a reality. Yes, the only thing that is stopping you from achieving your goals, dreams, and wishes is the limitations that you place in front of you. Think about it.

Do not worry about those dark pieces or vague spots of the puzzle—the tests and trials. They are part of the puzzle of life, but you can overcome them. Most of the time they are difficult, but they will not last. Sooner or later they will find their perfect fit or spot of importance. Sometimes we ourselves feel like we are on the dark spot or in the dark, but after a while we realize that, that point of time is very significant to our journey of life. At times, tough times and impossible situations may simply be an indication that you need to be flexible and be open to other possibilities. It could mean using another piece of the puzzle or trying out another spot; it may be time to change your thinking or use a new approach. It may take time, but somewhere, somehow, the piece of puzzle you are holding will finally fit into the whole picture.

When you get to the point of your limitations, the best thing to do is to seek God's guidance (which is best done actually from the beginning, not just when you are already desperate for help). Thank God that with Him it is never too late, and whenever you need Him he is just a call away. Also, do not hesitate to ask others for help. It is not always easy to ask for help, especially for someone who has been independent, but it is a wiser step than feeling sorry for yourself or giving up. Relax and stay calm. When you recover and regain your composure, you can refocus your attention on the three positive aspects of life mentioned earlier—your barn, your field of flowers, and your blue sky and white clouds. After a while, when you look once again at your life's puzzle, you will say, "Piece of cake."

Puzzles have continued to challenge and fascinate us for generations, just like life does. Just remember, a puzzle, like life, is meant to be put together patiently. At the end it brings out a fulfilling, beautiful masterpiece in *you*!

> *"Believe that life is worth living, and your belief will help create the fact."*
>
> William James, American psychologist and philosopher

The Secrets of Survival

Beyond the clouds, there is a blue sky. After the rain, there is sunshine. Tough times don't last and naturally disappear in time.

When life is going great, *celebrate*! When the going gets tough, the name of the game is *survive!* In my first book, *Today's S.O.S.* (Secrets of Survival), written in 1997, I gave many pointers in dealing with this life, managing available resources, and dealing with crisis situations. My personal life for the most part I would say has been beautiful! I continue to face challenges (face it, it is part of life), but not only do I persist to survive, but these challenging situations became my stepping stones. "Something good will come out of this." "Something good is about to happen!" When things are down, really down, the only way to go next is *up*.

Did you notice that I did not use the term *problem*? Instead I used *challenging situations*. Every problem, question, or situation must have an answer or solution. Some people easily give up saying, "It's too hard." "That's impossible!" "I can't do it!" And they quit. But if you believe it can be answered, you will find the solution. In both cases what was thought and declared will end up being the result. It is your positive attitude and/or thoughts, your faith that gives you the courage, intensity, diligence, and the determination to persevere until you find the answer or solution, until you reach your goal or destination.

If there is a will, there is a way.
When you think you can't, you can't.
When you think you can, YOU CAN!

Facing Tough Times: My Personal Survival Story

Sometimes I have people tell me, "Easy for you to say because you probably have not experienced real difficult times." I've found that this kind of thinking is common among people; they think they are the only one going through difficulties in life, and others are not. Some live with the victim mentality. On the contrary, all you need to do is get out of yourself for a moment, and you will notice that people around you all go through tough times. Tough times and life's challenges come in different shapes, degrees, intensities, and durations. I found out that tests, trials and tribulations are natural parts of our lives, and I have not found a single soul yet who is exempted, not even the royals or celebrities, who are supposed to have everything that they could ask for in life. So, let's be nice to one another, give each other a break, be more giving and forgiving. What is important is how we deal with or how we handle these tough situations when they come. Will you come out defeated or survive and WIN? Remember, most of these situations come without warning. It seems like no way you can prepare yourself for some totally unexpected challenges. How prepared or equipped you are in all aspects of your life—spiritually, mentally, emotionally, physically, socially, financially—can surely be of tremendous help to you. Don't even try to avoid these tests. You may not be able to, no matter what you do. Just have a different positive mindset to shield you as they arise. Just like mistakes and failures, these tough times could bring you closer to your destination. After all, *experience* is still the best teacher, and *practice* is the best trainer.

I personally have been through many trials. Some I admit were too difficult to bear. You feel like giving up. In my first book I shared a few, including being alone, away from home, losing a job, losing someone dear to me, facing death, and one most unexpected and unusual circumstance, which I will share with you here:

Being Homeless

"What is it like to be homeless?" I would never know the answer unless I experienced it myself, would I? Could it be possible? We were not expecting it, not even thinking of such a situation. But it happened.

We started doing interestingly well. After my husband and I searched to better ourselves on the financial field, we started our own business as an affiliate of a great company. We became very successful in our tender twenties. Ironically, when we hardly knew anything about business, nor did we have any experience. We just wanted to share the great discoveries we had. We had a good life when we were in Miami, our first home for ten years. With the great company, A.L. Williams, we realized the American dream, our own business, a big home, nice cars, luxurious trips, etc. We were living a lifestyle most people can only watch on TV, just like the *Lifestyles of the Rich and Famous*. We were not necessarily famous, but for us the lifestyle was way beyond our comprehension; it was more than we had ever dreamed of. It was wonderful, and we will continue to be appreciative of the leaders of that company for the wonderful experience.

That all changed, however, when we moved to California. The early nineties happened to be not the best time to make a move for business expansion and trying (while the company was making a merging transition), foolishly and naively, to maintain two homes and two offices in two far-apart states at the same time. Life became too tough to handle with the business. My husband decided to stop the business and go back to his profession, engineering. (You may call it a setback). We applied everything we had learned plus what our own experience had taught us. We were doing very well with our budgeting and planning. We felt we would be fine. This was a new beginning…

For a year my husband enjoyed his very good job. He liked it so much that he was prepared to retire with this company. His boss was preparing him to take over his position when he retired. It seemed like a stable job.

But the company, which had always been doing very well, started losing some big contracts and had to cut down. It so happened that my husband already finished his major projects when the company decided to freeze the remaining ones and resume when the company recovered. Since there was nothing for my husband to do and he was the newest person on board, his was the most logical position to cut.

My husband was laid off on his first anniversary year in July 1994. Since we had some emergency funds and could receive unemployment benefits, we did not worry at that time. He was good. I was confident he would find other employment soon. The company gave him a very good recommendation letter. Besides, we'd been through this before. This was the fourth time he'd been laid off. The first time was when we had just bought our first home and I had just delivered our first baby. Then he found another one, just to be laid off again and again (which in a way opened new doors to consider the business as an alternative). We were beginning to get used to it and felt we would make it. We were still young, confident of the opportunities and our willingness to work hard to whatever came our way.

By October there was still no job, and our emergency fund was running out. As if that was not enough, he heard from his sister that she was going to have chemotherapy again after her left breast had already been removed over a year ago. This time her condition seemed worse, and she refused more treatment. My in-laws, who'd just returned from their vacation, had to go back for her. My husband wanted to join them, but we could only raise what my in-laws needed for their trip. We prayed for her day and night. A month later we were told that she passed away at the hospital. It was a big blow to her family, to us, and particularly to my husband, who was not able to go home to see her while she was still alive. It was very difficult to take. She was a wonderful person, only thirty-two years old, a mother of a beautiful two-year-old girl.

By Thanksgiving we had completely run out of resources. Our friends and churchmates started bringing us food, including a turkey for Thanksgiving and a ham for Christmas. They were our extended family, and we were grateful for them. Employers seemed to freeze up their hiring during the holiday season, at a time when we needed the work the most. In January we started packing our things. We knew that unless we got a job, we would not be able to pay the next month's rent. We notified the owner that if that were the case, we were ready to vacate the house so he could rent it to someone else. We did not like the idea of being evicted.

The first week of February 1995 we held a move-out sale. We sold all our furniture and just about everything we had. We had no place to put them anyway. Storage had become so expensive. We took just a few clothes, our valuable papers and memorable items, whatever we could fit into our van. Amazingly the sun came out for the first time in winter that weekend. A lot of people came as they noticed the "MOVING SALE" sign—probably the first of the season. We sold a lot, one of the most successful garage sales ever. Close to two thousand dollars was generated. The following day more was sold. We gave away a lot, too. Salvation Army picked up the rest of what was remaining, which was still plenty. They were delighted. It is amazing how much stuff we accumulated and did not use or need after all. We were very thankful for the turn out. It would help us survive until a job could come along.

We thought of using the money to pay the house rent. But if we did, the next month could be a problem again, and we would not have anything left for food and other necessities. We decided to move ahead with our plan. The question now was, "Where will we go?"

Prior to this, I was a program coordinator with an education and resource center, a community outreach program whose purpose was to help individuals and families get needed information, support, and resources to help them. I never thought it could personally help me, too. I actually gained knowledge of resources available for people of our predicament, which helped immensely. I had everything planned out, which I thought was better than feeling depressed and hopeless. If we would go along with our plan, it would buy us needed time until we could get back on our feet again.

I heard of a short-term transition homeless shelter in our city. I drove there to see it. It was not bad. It was almost new, beautiful, and very spacious. I was actually amazed how nice it was. I visited others prior, and I knew my husband and children would rather sleep in the van, which we were ready to do. I called to tell them of our situation and asked if they could help us out temporarily. The people at the shelter were very understanding, especially knowing that there were young children involved. Our children's ages at that time were twelve, ten, and nine. But as much as they wanted to help us, nearly a hundred other people were calling each day for help, too. So we were placed on a waiting list. I was instructed to call up each Monday to follow up and see if any openings were available.

Before we left our house, I received a call from the school nurse to inform me of my son's eye test result. He needed to have a doctor's checkup and probably needed eyeglasses. I thanked the nurse for informing me but could not tell her that we no longer had health insurance and could not afford extra expenses like the doctor's visit and eyeglasses. Out of desperation I thought of a resource, the county social services office. *No, not there, please!* I said to myself. But as a parent, I would do anything for my children. It is hard to describe how I felt when I went there and lined up with the others, all sorts of people in that very long line. For a while I forgot about my self-consciousness. I've never seen such a variety of people in my life. My focus went to watching all these people around me. There were mothers with babies, old people, people of all ages, all colors, all types of faces. I felt I discovered so many things I would never have known had I not gone to that office. The place was very crowded. A guard said it was like that every day, sometimes worse. (By the way, this was over ten years ago. Can you imagine how it is now?) When my turn came, I told the social worker I was applying for medical assistance for my son because the school nurse suggested he needed a checkup and maybe eyeglasses. As if there were still some pride left in me that I hesitated to ask for real help. Nevertheless, she asked about our situation and asked me to fill out a bunch of papers. By the time I was finished, she was telling me that our whole family would receive Medicaid benefits, a monthly check of about eight hundred dollars, along with food stamps. She had a look in her eyes that seemed to say, "You don't have to say it. I know, and I understand." All she said was, "It is really tough nowadays. You are not alone."

I was overwhelmed. Should I say, "No" or just say, "Thank you!" That was one very special day, which I will never forget.

The second week of February we left our rented home. My husband still had no job, and there was no availability yet at the shelter. The check we would temporarily receive from the county was not enough to get us an apartment, and the waiting list for more affordable ones was very long. As much as I did not want to, for the sake of my children, I called my aunt. I told her it would only be about a month while we were waiting for housing, not knowing that I was referring to a shelter. She and her family welcomed us. I honored my promise. We were out of there in exactly a month. She did not know that we were actually going to a motel where we could stay on a weekly basis. It was small, very old, and not well kept, but it was private, and we had our own

TV and bathroom. We noticed other families around us that we could recognize as being in the same boat as we were.

During this rough moment of our life together, I knew I had to temporarily take charge. It was just too much for my husband to handle his grief over his sister's death, his job search, and this. I told him not to worry and just concentrate on looking for work. This was the time I was able to exercise my *resourcefulness* to the fullest. What kept me going was the knowledge that somehow this was all *temporary*.

Thank God my husband finally got a job in mid-March, just in time, as we were about to run out of money again. We were definitely not ready to apply for a rental house, but we were able to maintain daily necessities like food and gas. We managed to keep paying for our car and insurance payment. I continued to follow up on the shelter. It would help us save enough money so we could start all over again, which was actually the purpose of the shelter. Our welfare benefit ended one month after my husband started working. We are very thankful for such a program for citizens in need. It was brief and only temporary but just enough to help us. It actually made a real difference in our lives.

In late March we moved into the homeless transition shelter. We met all kinds of people there. Some seemed fine. Some you would like to take some caution. There were two sections: families on the left side, singles on the right. We, of course, stayed in the family section. It had a common family room with a TV, comfortable sofas and chairs, and plenty of toys for children of all ages. There was even a library with sets of encyclopedias and computers. Since the children continued to go to school, it was handy. There was a common patio and a common dining room where volunteers came on rotation to cook for us and sometimes even serve us at our tables. It turned out to be a very impressive, thoughtful effort of the founders, workers, and volunteers of the shelter to try to preserve the human dignity left on these homeless people.

The shelter was situated on a good-sized property alongside a creek with a view of the mountain. It had a laundry room, which could be used on a scheduled basis. The shelter was run with strict but reasonable rules that included a curfew and sharing some chores like dishwashing and vacuuming. Everything was provided for free, including soap, toothbrush, toothpaste, and toilet paper, which were donated by nearby churches, businesses, and generous people. The idea was not to spoil the residents, but to help them save as much money as they could so they could move out faster. They were very thoughtful of the children's needs, providing them with lots of toys and a schedule of interesting activities for the children to do while the parents were attending community meetings or enrichment training in the evenings.

It was almost a perfect place for those who did not have any place to go. Some people did not want to leave. They began to feel so comfortable and secure in the shelter that going back to the real world became scary. As people constantly went in and out, we met some wonderful people whom we never thought would be in such a place, just like we were there. Some residents wondered about us when we went out in our custom van, which was paid off, or in our Volvo. This just showed that our situation could happen to anybody. Some residents who seemed hopeless bounced back and did well all over again, ready to go back to the mainstream of the society. And the others who were also given all the chances but the terms of stay were not satisfied and were finally asked to leave; you wonder how they could continue to live out there. It was sadder in the case where there were children involved. We wondered how those children would live and grow. What will their future be like? Seeing them for a while, I could not help but be concerned. I sometimes spent my nights thinking about and praying for them. "If I were only in a position to help…"

I almost failed to mention what was inside our assigned room, which was like the other rooms there. It was a comfortable space, much like the size of a motel room, with tiled floor where we put down an area rug. There was a nice bathroom with an oversized bathtub and a modern toilet. It actually was a lot better than the motel we stayed in. Since there were five of us, we were given two bunk beds, one with double size below. They were complete with mattresses, bed sheets, blankets, bedcovers, and pillows. Even towels were provided, which we truly appreciated, but we decided to use our own. I arranged the room well and put some stuffed animals on the bed to make the atmosphere more like home. When I picked up the children at school to show them where we would be staying next, they were not thrilled to be there but eventually adjusted to it as I told them it would only be temporary and would be a "unique learning experience." God must have a purpose for us, and we had to make the most of it while we were there.

My husband eventually accepted the place also and liked the idea of our plan for recovery. The counselor assigned to us was wonderful. She was understanding, supportive, and very helpful. It truly was a special place. They even let us have our fish tank, which we eventually left in the reception room so others could continue to enjoy it; watching the fish swim is somehow very relaxing and therapeutic. When we were in our room, we felt like it was ours, our own comfortable, cozy home. We had fun playing lots of different games. We had plenty of quality family time. We also prayed together a lot. We were truly grateful to everyone at the shelter for providing us with such a pleasant, dignified place to stay.

I used to think of homelessness as a horrible experience. It can be for some. Although some moments were undesirable, in totality we actually had a very nice time there. Our children played with other kids, and one time our youngest child said, "I like it here. You get to have a lot of friends, lots of fun…it is like a very big family." The other two responded, "Me, too." I was stunned. The place that I initially feared might traumatize my children psychologically turned out to be an experience they could treasure. We all learned a lot about other people, their ways of living, how they got there, some of their very sad backgrounds, and their means of survival. Things we would have never had an idea about if we had not been there. I found a great purpose in our stay there. The homeless shelter was about PEOPLE, and the experience enriched our lives immeasurably.

Our four-month stay ended when we raised enough money to pay the first month's rent and deposit on a modest four-bedroom house across from the school we desired. Our plan was delayed a month due to major repairs, new tires, and registration for both cars, which we were glad were taken cared of before we moved out. It was a perfect home for us, which would include my in-laws, who had stayed with their other relatives for a while. We were a family again and in our home once more.

We were so happy and are still grateful to everyone who helped us as we went through this unusual experience in life. We thank God for the path of life He gave us and for the miracles He continues to show us each day, for the assurance that wherever we are, whatever we are going through, He is always with us.

I found out that homelessness does not only happen to just "lazy bums," as some people call homeless individuals. It happens and can still happen to *anyone*. Statistics show tens of thousands of people homeless in every major city and over a million nationwide, about a fourth of which are our veterans. It happens not only to the low-income earners but also to former executives, professors, lawyers, and other professionals who used to have great jobs or businesses, expensive homes, and great reputations. Some not only lose their jobs and homes but also their families and their sense of dignity and pride.

It amazed me to go out each day and recognize the faces of those in the shelter just about every place we went—in grocery stores, shopping malls, parks, theater, at church, etc. Some actually have jobs and look decent. My family also began to notice cars or vans that were full of personal belongings and recognized those who were either vacationing or homeless also. There are so many people out there who need help but just don't know where to go or are too embarrassed to seek help from others. Some are justified of their hesitation to be rejected or be snubbed again.

Yet there is nothing really to be ashamed about. Homelessness is not a sin or a crime. It has now become a possible part of our lives, as thousands of people continue to lose their jobs or their businesses. At the point of writing this, America is experiencing what is being referred to as "foreclosure tsunami," and all kinds of challenges are becoming a serious concern of every citizen in all sectors of our society. According to the 2006 US Census Bureau report, our estimated 78.2 million Baby Boomers, the generation born between 1946 and 1964, are now retiring at a rate of about 8,000 per day, about 330 every hour. Currently there are about 3.3 workers for each Social Security beneficiary. This is not mentioning the natural and manmade disasters that we citizens are being asked to always be prepared for. Can you picture the situation we are in?

If you or someone you know is going through tough times, be assured, YOU ARE NOT ALONE. And it is not the end of the world either. Do not give up. Don't wait until the last minute when worse things could happen before doing something. There are many resources available for temporary help. Both government-funded and private non-profit services and agencies can be sought. Look in the first pages of your phone book under government pages or community resources for names like *Social Services, United Way,* and *Salvation Army.* Also, you may refer to the inside back cover of this book for a quick reference. Keep making phone calls until you reach the help that you need.

Everyone should know about these things. It may not be you. It may not be now. It may be someone you can help later. You may be able to help save some lives as well.

A home is not just a building that we rent or buy. A home is wherever we can find rest and security. A home is where your heart is. When you find a meaningful relationship with your God, with your family, with other people, or even yourself, you are *at home*.

Mistakes and Failures are Helpful

"Those things that hurt instruct."
Benjamin Franklin

Do you know of anyone who has not made a mistake? Nobody. In one way or another, each one of us has made mistakes and is likely to make some more. A *mistake* is an error in action, judgment, perception, or understanding. It is a natural *part* of life. It is a part of our *learning process*, the purpose of mistakes, especially for those of us who learn better the hard way. This should not make us feel down or like total failures. If we look at each mistake and failure more positively and learn the lesson from them, in the end we will see these as great necessities that help us grow and mature to become better people. That is what *hands-on* and *learning from experience* is all about.

We always hear that everybody makes mistakes. That is true, and no one is exempt. So why do we feel so down on ourselves when we are obviously not alone in this situation? Is it not simply because of our feeling of embarrassment or fear of humiliation or rejection that we even try to hide it? Of course it hurts. It can be very painful and demeaning at times. But what is there to be ashamed about?

When I was a child, my father used to tell us, "There is nothing to be ashamed about poverty and honest mistakes. The only time you should be ashamed is when you did something wrong." These words, first of all, gave me some clarification of the term. A mistake is unintentional.

After all, who would be crazy enough to do something that he or she already knew was not right and would not work or would only result in disaster? Well, some people still do. That is not a mistake. That is a willful wrongdoing for whatever purpose and result they are trying to accomplish. They cannot escape from the natural cause and effect rule though. Sooner or later, whatever is sown, that will be reaped also. It never fails.

So, you wonder why people continue to do wrong. Don't they know the clear path warning? Should we include this in our invisible life path manual? WARNING: "Wrongdoing is an offense with corresponding severe penalties. Any violator will not go unpunished." An offender may manage to get away from the court, but our nature has its own way of making sure that justice is done. Whether you like it or not, that is the truth. Accept it or not, that is the way our life on earth operates.

We can prevent wrongdoing. We have a free will to choose to do right or to do wrong. It is up to us to make a decision and make a choice. We are very capable of doing what we choose or decide to do once we put our minds to it.

Since a mistake is unintentional and we have no prior knowledge of what the outcome will be, it is difficult to avoid mistakes as we subject ourselves to daily trials and errors. You are actually taking a chance. You are in the process of learning to find out later if your theory or your gut feeling is right or wrong. Do not be afraid of your mistakes. On the other hand, you can take some precautions and try to prevent any unnecessary mistakes. Reading, researching, and simply asking questions first to verify and increase your knowledge on the subject matter can be very important preventive measures and are valuable tools to the learning process.

FAILURES? Same thing. In fact, come to think of it, there is really no such thing as failure. It is just a negative connotation created by those people who have little understanding and yet love to condemn and put down people. Why be bothered by them? They are surely no help anyway. Sure we make mistakes. Some people consider that a failure. That is why they sometimes quit. But if we stop focusing on the mistake or failure, learn from it, and move ahead, then we can do better next time, and we will finally succeed, grow, and develop into better, more mature individuals.

Wise people say, *"Mistakes and failures can either break you or mold you."* That is true, but I prefer to say that it should not break you at all. So, the only time we actually fail is when we quit or give up. Do not give up. There are still a lot of great chances, better opportunities, and brighter days ahead of you. Every day you wake up is a new beginning. There are still plenty of doors for you to open.

How do I know? I am already an expert. I've already committed countless mistakes and, as some people say, "failed" so many times. After all that I have been through, it is truly a miracle I am still up, alive, and excited about life. Most importantly, you can survive these mistakes and failures, too.

"Anyone who has never made a mistake has never tried anything new."

Albert Einstein, German-born American physicist

"Far better it is to dare mighty things, to win glorious triumphs, even though checkered by failure, than to take rank with those poor spirit who neither enjoy much nor suffer much, because they live in the gray twilight that knows not victory or defeat."

Theodore Roosevelt

"Some of the best lessons we ever learn, we learn from our mistakes and failures. The error of the past is the success and wisdom of the future."

Tyron Edwards, American theologian

Overcoming Handicaps and Disabilities

Whenever referring to another person, an individual, a human being, or whatever we prefer to call ourselves, it is interesting how we come out with words like "normal," "abnormal," "disabled," or "handicapped." But then no one can give a plain, clear definition or basis for what is considered normal.

I remember how I agonized as a child, feeling abnormal, unusual, a feeling that I am quite different from the others. I happened to be a very tall girl, way taller than everybody else, including boys. That gave me an inferiority complex. I struggled to bend my knees under my long skirt, and I almost developed a hunch back trying to appear shorter. What I didn't realize was that the shortest among us felt the same way, same with the one with the darkest color, or the one with a shorter leg, or the one with big ears. I also found out later why my neighbor did not continue going to school. She was afraid to be laughed at for "not being smart" and having to stutter in her speech.

As I grew up, however, I found out that there was really nothing wrong about being tall. Come to realize (thanks to the encouragement of my close family and friends), models and beauty contestants are mostly tall girls. Being tall has a lot of advantages, like reaching for things. All of a sudden, my abnormality became an asset. Amazingly I found out that there are even girls and women in this world who are taller than me. Isn't it funny that I agonized for so long all for nothing?

And that is just one of my many handicaps or defects. Just to name a few more, one of my ears can't hear very well, and there is a tiny cave-like hole on the back of it, which I tried to hide for so many years. But today it does not bother me anymore. I am no longer embarrassed to ask someone to repeat what was just said. I learned that I just have to deal with it. Also, I did not grow up with television and books, so I am very poor in English, but I am no longer ashamed to admit that. Before, I hardly talked because I was concerned that people would laugh at me, but an American friend assured me, "It is all right. Don't worry about it. They won't laugh at you. The more you should practice so that you can improve." I appreciated my friend's understanding and encouraging words. It helped a lot.

Through all these years, I have made a startling discovery that *everybody* actually has some form of a defect, a handicap, a disability, or whatever you might call an imperfection. Some just happen to be more obvious than others. Could it be that these are just part of our *uniqueness*, each of us having to be different from one another? After years of meeting and observing people, I have drawn my own conclusion that we all actually have abnormalities, handicaps, or imperfections simply because *nobody is perfect.* Consider my point. It is reassuring then to say that whatever it is that is unnecessarily hindering us from feeling normal or limiting us from feeling all right should be faced and accepted as simply a part of our uniqueness. My handicaps and disabilities are normal, thank God!

Nobody is perfect, and *no one* has a perfect life. That is an accepted fact. It is just a matter of how we let our imperfections put a limit on how we enjoy our lives; how we allow ourselves or others to put limitations on how we should live. Enough! Just face it, accept it, deal with it, and make the most out of it. And I am not just talking about physical terms but mental, emotional, and financial terms as well. We cannot say that the smartest guy is the happiest, nor can we say that the simplest gal can't find happiness or a person with perfect vision is always happier than a blind person. Can we? Poverty does not necessarily hinder others from being fulfilled.

Turn your negatives into positives. Make it an asset or advantage. If we develop such an attitude and belief level, later on we can say, "In spite of my imperfection, I will live my life to the fullest…no matter what. I am grateful for what I am and what I have, and that is a lot to live for." When you do you will then begin to discover what VICTORY means.

> "No one can make you feel inferior without your consent."
>
> Eleanor Roosevelt

> "A positive thinker does not refuse to recognize the negative, he refuses to dwell on it. Positive thinking is a form of thought which habitually looks for the best results from the worst conditions."
>
> Norman Vincent Peale, American writer and minister

*"Kindness is the language which the deaf
can hear and the blind can see."*
Mark Twain

The Problem Solving Process

*"If there was nothing wrong in the world,
there wouldn't be anything for us to do."*
George Bernard Shaw,
Irish essayist

Yes, there is a better way for you to handle your problems, instead of your problems handling you and your life!

Do you have problems? Of course! Who does not have one?

We always hear that *nobody is perfect*. And as we've established, *nobody's life is perfect*. So what then is the point of feeling sorry for yourself when you are not alone? Everyone has his or her own problems, maybe worse than yours. Out of all the people you know, how many know your problem? One? Two? Nobody? So everybody else is thinking, *Lucky you. You are perfectly fine. You have no problems.* They just don't know. And you are probably thinking the same thing about those around you, which is why you are thinking that you are the only one who has such a huge problem. Just like mistakes, nobody wants to talk about them; we do not announce our problems to the world. What is the real problem here?

The problem is…the word is so misused or overused that we think of a *problem* as something dreadful. Just hearing or thinking of the word makes some people perceive it as *a disaster*. The word has gained such a bad reputation that we misuse it on just about everything and every situation we encounter—problem with the weather, cars, traffic, work, school, kids, pets, money, etc. It is insane! Have we forgotten our school days when the word *problem* was used interchangeably with words such as *hypothesis, question,* or *situation,* meaning, "We are confronted with a perplexing or puzzling question, idea, or situation that just needs to be studied or analyzed to derive a more concrete answer or solution"? That is no big deal. It is positive. That is where the *challenge* comes from, a part of our life process.

Another issue is that we linger too much on the perceived problems that get us down. Why not *focus on* the *solutions* and ways to resolve things or improve the situation instead.

Situations come to us every day to keep us from getting bored and to get us into doing something meaningful and productive. These situations will never go away as long as we live. So why not take them as welcome partners in life? Why not look at problems as *situations, questions, or ideas,* whichever is more applicable. That may help change our perspectives and help us to deal with these problems better. Another way is, instead of being *in* the box, totally involved with the situation, it may help to look at situations from *outside* the box to see things more objectively.

I remember a friend who spoke at a seminar in Miami, Florida, who said to the audience, *"Problems will always be there. But you know what? If your attitude is right, you got no problem!"* What problem?

I actually learned this problem-solving process when I was a nursing student. I am pretty sure that other courses or professions have a similar version, too. As professional nurses, we apply this process to our patient care plans when we approach a problem we have identified with our patients and clients. It is a very important and helpful tool that the health team uses every day at the hospital, clinic, or in the field.

Little did I know that I can also use it in my everyday life, not only at work but at home, in my marriage, in raising our children, dealing with other people, and in other various situations. It is practical and very helpful, as it taught me to slow down and look into the situation first before I jump to any conclusion or commit to any drastic action. It has become so valuable to me and my family that I thought I would share it with you. Here are the five steps in problem solving:

1. *Identify* the Problem (or Situation) – Be specific.
2. *Analyze* the Problem – Assess or examine the underlying factors or circumstances that may be contributing to the problem.

3. *Formulate a Plan of Action* – Make a goal or objective to cure or resolve the identified problem. List specific actions toward accomplishing that goal.
4. *Intervene/Implement* – Do it! Do or act as planned to possibly solve the problem and expect a good result.
5. *Evaluate* – Assess the effectiveness of the action plan and intervention. If it is effective, good for you! If not, start the process again; try other possibilities and alternatives for solutions. Included here are considerations for *preventive measures*, to avoid the reoccurrence of the same problem.

Example #1:
   A. Problem: Husband not feeling well/stress at work. This could be treated as two separate problems, but since they are interrelated we will for now treat them as one.

   B. Analysis:
      1. He is complaining of not feeling well, and it shows.
      2. He loves his job, and it pays well, but it can be very demanding.
      3. We have not had a vacation for quite a while. Maybe it's time for one.
      4. I know some of the things that helped him in the past. Maybe it's time to reinforce them.

   C. Plan of Action:
      1. Take his vital signs and call the doctor for an appointment if necessary.
      2. Time to remind him of using relaxation techniques at work.
      3. Discuss a vacation idea with him, and if he agrees, arrange a date and start planning.
      4. Have a meeting with the children to agree to provide the most restful environment at home and lots of TLC (tender loving care).

   D. Intervention: Will do exactly as planned!

E. Evaluation: Knowing my husband well, that should do it.

Let's take a look at another example and a different situation:

Example #2:

F. Problem: *Losing a job*. Yes, you just learned you are now jobless. (I can share this with you since my husband and I have personally experienced this kind of situation, not once but several times.)

G. Analysis:
    1. There must be a *reason* why you were laid off (or worse, unreasonably fired). If you were *laid off*, consider that the company may have no other choice (i.e., they could be losing money or on the verge of closing their business unless they do something). If you were *fired*, be reasonable. There may be something to learn from it or something to be thankful for eventually.
    2. The affect on you (and your family) of not having a paycheck: not being able to pay the bills or buy basic necessities. You're seeing the disaster! But if you look further, you may discover that there is actually a light at the end of the tunnel. Don't rush into conclusions or drastic actions that you may regret later. Just about everyone experiences trying events like this, and these people survived and did even better afterward. You are not alone, and there is always hope, a solution, and a brighter tomorrow.

H. Plan of action:
    1. Take into consideration your company's condition, why they have to lay off people. They may not want to lay off anybody, but the business is maybe going through tough times. Don't take it personally. They have to do what they have to do. If you were to find

The Secrets of Survival

a better and higher paying job, you would probably not hesitate to say goodbye also. If you were fired, either that company does not deserve you, or there may be a lesson that you can learn from this. When one door closes, a better one opens. Find another perfect match that can better appreciate your talents and contributions. Make plans for survival in the mean time, while you are looking for another job.

2. Again, the name of the game is SURVIVAL! The game of survival directs us *to do whatever it takes* in order to survive in a more constructive way. (Helpful tips can be found throughout this book.) It may be difficult for a while, but if you remain up and continue moving, looking, persevering, and praying, eventually the tough times will pass.

I. Implementation:
   1. Get up and get out! There is another job out there waiting for you. If you will use your previous experiences as a learning process, that will lead you to become more mature and wiser in looking for better opportunities.
   2. Keep looking. Send your resumes. There is plenty of support and lots of services available if you need help with your resume or job search.
   3. Stretch your remaining budget. Ask for help if necessary. Learn to better prepare yourself next time; something like this has to happen again. Remember, during your most difficult times, when it seems as if nothing and nobody else can help, God can be there to carry you through.

J. Evaluation: The actions you take will determine the outcome. Whatever the situation, don't lose hope or quit. Learn from every circumstance. It will make you stronger. Finally, brighter days may be just moments away.

See, the *problem-solving process* is really that simple. It should not be mistaken with the term "Crisis Intervention," unless you are facing a true crisis. It is as simple as baking a cake; you start with just a box of flour and a recipe. Get the ingredients and mix them together. Then you cook it, and presto! You have a wonderful dessert. It is like a student dealing with an assignment that begins with a perplexing question or problem. He gathers his tools to look for the answer, experiments, verifies, finally writing down his best answer, then presto! An A+!

Just like a husband and wife, who normally argue and fight during the early years of their marriage while getting to know each other better and adjusting to each other's personalities; they learn to calm down and listen to each other, have heart to heart talks, and make up (actually, this is the best part and adds great spice to a marriage). The process applies to any given situation and is a better way of handling conflicts. If practiced by both parties, they can communicate more objectively and come up with better resolutions they can both be happy with.

Learn to focus on the *solution*, not the problem. When you practice this process, it is amazing how much you can learn. The most important lesson to learn is to eventually realize that what you are really facing is not a problem but a *situation* that can be resolved. Take it as *a challenge*. Experience how good it feels to be able to say at the end, "Mission accomplished!"

As I previously mentioned, you can use the same above principle to any given situation, challenge, or question. You just need to modify or make adjustment to the name and circumstance. Here's an example which we will call…

The Dream Achievement Process

"Dreams are extremely important. You can't do it unless you imagine it."

George Lucas, American film maker

1. *Identify/ Visualize.* Crystallize or create a clear picture of your *dream, goal, or idea*. It can be a drawing, a picture, or in writing. The more specific you are with the details, target dates, locations, etc., the better.
2. *Analyze/Examine.* Explore the possibilities, meaning, purpose, desired outcome. Make sure this is what you really want to achieve or accomplish in life. Something that you can believe in, make a commitment to devote time, energy, and other resources needed to achieve it. Something that you will value and can make you real happy. Do you have that burning *desire* to make it happen?
3. Create a *Plan of Action*. Without the action you are just dreaming or wishing. You have to be determined to make it happen. Outline your plan, the road map, and your strategies. Gather the tools and supplies needed. Gather your team if needed.
4. *Implementation/ Take Action.* Do It! Execute the plan. Be persistent. Never quit. *Make things happen.*
5. *Evaluate/ Enjoy* the result of desired reward!

"All dreams can come true – if we have the courage to pursue them."

Walt Disney

Just keep practicing this process. It works! The usual advice you will hear is start small until you become more comfortable, until you are ready for big things. That is true on most cases. But in case you suddenly have this big dream, as you go through the process and you believe enough that you are ready to accomplish it, no need to procrastinate. Go for it!

Yes! The Secrets Work!

Remember that the only limitations you have are the limitations you put in front of you. Otherwise the sky is the limit, meaning your opportunity is as UNLIMITED as the *universe*!

Once you grasp these principles, you will live your life with unlimited joy and excitement. This time you can call your name followed by a loud, "Go for it!" Let's move mountains!

> *"Believe you can, and you can. Belief is one of the most powerful of all problem dissolvers. When you believe that a difficulty can be overcome, you are more than halfway to victory over it already."*
>
> Norman Vincent Peale,
> American writer and minister

> *"We must accept finite disappointment, but we must never lose infinite hope."*
>
> Martin Luther King, American Civil Rights leader and minister

> *"The future belongs to those who believe in the beauty of their dreams."*
>
> Eleanor Roosevelt, former first lady, USA, writer, diplomat

The Secrets of the Wealthy

> *"Wealth is not in making money, but in making the man while he is making money."*
>
> John Wicker, American artist

Three Ways to Make Money

1. YOU at work.
2. Your MONEY at work.
3. DEPENDENCE on somebody else.

Why be poor if you can be wealthy?
Why be dependent if you can be independent?

> *"Give a man a fish and he will eat for a day. Teach him how to fish and he will eat for a lifetime"*
>
> Chinese Proverb

Are you *earning a living* or *living a life*? Here we will examine why some people continue to work so hard just to maintain a living while some after the hard work and applying the discovered secrets are eventually barely working to live a life.

Besides knowing and living the secret of the law of attraction, technically, the secrets of the wealthy are summarized by these three words:

```
        LEVERAGE
           /\
          /  \
         /____\
   TAXES      INVESTMENT
```

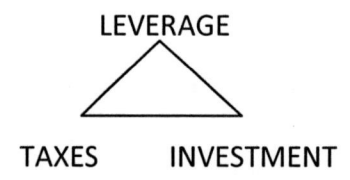

The wealthy people are very good at managing their money, and the amount does not have to be huge. They know how to save money in many ways (but not the kind that you just set aside, not doing anything or earning). They know the tax laws and are smart enough to have tax experts on their side to maximize their tax benefits. They know how and where to invest.

The main thing that made most of them very wealthy, besides what they refer to as pure luck or being at the right place at the right time, is they understand *how money works*! Even better is *how money can work for them*! They understand *leverage*, maximizing the result even with very little time, money, or effort of their own. They use OPM, OPT, OPE: other people's money, time/talent and effort to their benefit. No, they are not trying to take advantage of people. They are simply applying this one great principle: Work smarter, not harder. Leverage.

Let's get into the practical side of what this looks like. As an individual you can only work one to two jobs and work eight to sixteen hours per day then go home dead tired, right? The maximum that you can get paid is the number of hours x the amount you are getting paid per hour. For example, $15/hour x 16 hours = $240. That's it! You cannot possibly work any more hours to get more pay. Then you cry with the taxes you have to pay with that. Now, here is your boss who, let's say, has 100 employees. For him it is better that even he only makes $10 per person he is paying $120 to $240 per day; when you multiply that $10 by 100 = $1,000 for him to make each day. The best part is he can make that money even he only shows up for an hour or even while taking a vacation. Wouldn't you love to have that kind of job…or life? If you do, would you like to know *how* you, too, can do the same? Well, it is time that you take financial learning more seriously before you jump onto this wonderful secret bandwagon.

The thing is you cannot be mad with these rich or wealthy people. Why? First, it is interesting to know that the majority of these wealthy people also started broke or as average and ordinary like you and me.

Second, the information or knowledge they have, the tax benefits that they are enjoying, the investments they do, and the leveraging they are utilizing are all available for you also! If you don't know, then you are not able to exercise and benefit from it. Just like you may have a huge inheritance somewhere, but if you don't know, how will you enjoy it? (It is amazing to find out how much unclaimed riches are out there.) Then it will be your mission to imagine what is it like if you have what you really want in life. What will you be doing if you have the wealth you are desiring right in your hand or your fat bank account? Can you imagine it? Can you see your dream as if it is real? Now, your next mission is to inform and equip yourself of the knowledge and means needed to get to the realization of your dream.

Let me share with you one great formula I learned over twenty years ago. Most people are not aware that this simple formula can have a tremendous impact on their finances. It is called the *Rule of 72*, or the *"Banker's Rule."* Don't be surprised if the employees in the bank cannot explain it to you or do not know about it at all. It is one of the best kept secrets that banks owners and executives prefer people never get to know. It is vital information that everyone should be aware of, and when you find out how simple it is that even elementary students could easily understand, it makes you wonder why it is never taught in our schools. It could have made a big difference in the lives of many.

Rule of 72

Formula: 72 ÷ ____% = ____ years to double your money

This simple formula can show you how money can work harder for you or the bank. Take the number seventy-two, divide it by the percentage of interest being applied to your savings, investment or credit, and this will give you the number of years to double that money. For example, say you have $10,000 hidden in one of your drawers, not making any interest at all; instead it is losing its value because of inflation (losing its buying power). You decide to bring it to the bank, a place we are programmed to think is the best and safest place to put our money. Did you really think these banks with their huge fancy buildings opened up their businesses just to serve you? Why then are they charging you more for just about every little service you need? Of course, they are big businesses! And you did not think for a minute that all the money you are faithfully depositing in them is just sitting in their vaults waiting for you to withdraw, right? Of course not! They are investing it. No, not for you, for them! Take a look at this and consider:

Illustration: *(Applying the Rule of 72)*

$$72 \div \_\_\_\% = \_\_\_\_\_ \text{ years to double your money}$$

Example using your $10,000:

	6 years	12	18	24	30	36
2%						$20,000
6%		$20,000		$40,000		$80,000
12%	$20,000	$40,000	$80,000	$160,000	$320,000	$640,000
24%	$40K	$160K	$640K	$2.5M		

That is why it is called the *"Magic of Compound Interest."* It works like magic! The bank customers are being given from .2% to 2%. Some with large deposits are happy and proud to get 6% to 12%! Compare that to how much the banks or lenders can make (which you can also make if you know how) over the amount they are giving the customers. Don't you think it will be wise for you to learn and master using this formula from here on? Now grab your calculator and calculate how much at 24% on the two remaining blanks, the 30th and 36th years. WOW! Isn't that amazing? If people only know about this earlier in life, parents can have better financial strategies for their future and their children's futures. It will make a big difference to the money management of those who are getting inheritances or winning big on a game, don't you think? People will have better opportunities to invest or better manage what they have and have a better plan for a brighter future for them and their loved ones.

The more you grasp and practice the principle and *the power of duplication and multiplication* in financial and business terms, the better your career and life will be. This is really very simple. The farmers understood and practiced this principle for ages when they were planting those small seeds. Countless networkers became very successful or wealthy applying the same. Try this one and test your knowledge so far. If I offer you $100,000 right now versus a penny doubling itself every day for the next thirty days, which one will you take? Do your math and be amazed of how powerful compounding interest works, as Albert Einstein, the genius who formulated the Rule of 72, expressed so long ago. If you will, share with me what you came up with. If you read this far and respond to this, I am reserving surprise rewards for the top ten with the best answers. Make the Rule of 72 and *leveraging* work for you!

If anyone thinks that the government has all the answers and solutions, think again. Do yourself a big favor. It is time to be aware of what's going on, to learn some secrets that will benefit you also. It is WAKE UP TIME! Read your Social Security statement, if you are receiving one, and share it, discuss it with as many people as you can think of whom you care about. All the information and warnings you need are right there: *"Social Security can't do it all. You also will need other savings, investments, pensions, or retirement accounts to make sure you have enough money to live comfortably when you retire."* Of course, most people say, "I don't have money now. Where will I get the money to save for my retirement?" If you are making this kind of comment, and you are still young and strong, then you know that you are in big trouble already (before you even get old), unless you do something to change that. Can you imagine about 90% of our nation's population dependent on our government, if not their relatives or charity? Of course, it is a nightmare to think about it. It is like imagining a drained lake or reservoir or a drought. It is now becoming more difficult for me to imagine young families giving their best to raise their young children and sometimes taking care of their parents' retirement needs as well. With all the demands and financial burdens going with these responsibilities, how do they make it? How do people nowadays survive? Can you imagine America as another third world country? Something needs to be done before it is too late, wouldn't you agree?

The task cannot be done by the government alone, nor can it be done by any single or few individuals or group or organization. But if *each* and *every one* of us does our part, then we can make a difference. *You* have to do your part; *I* have to do my part; *everyone* has to do his or her part. Someone came up with a great acronym for the word T.E.A.M.: Together Each Accomplishes More.

If you have the right information, anyone regardless of age, sex, educational, social, or economic background, can be financially independent! And that is great news! And on most cases, it does not have to take a lifetime, in contrast to most who have lived their entire lives only dreaming about being financially independent but never accomplish it. It has been proven many times that it can be done more or less in 2-5 years (could be sooner or later than that depending on the commitment of the individual), much better than the 40-50 years plan that our system has in place, and still 96% of our baby boomers are retiring broke.

If anybody can, why only few, less than 5%, are financially independent? The opportunity is available to everyone, but it is not achieved by everybody. Why? Because there are qualifications involved. Yes, *information* is vital, like going to college to be a doctor, a lawyer, or engineer, you actually can study how to be rich or financially secure. You may have read this whole book, accumulated so many other books on how to be successful or financially independent, and even attended all success seminars, but if you are *full of excuses* (like no time, no money), missing the necessary ingredients to succeed, you may end up one of the huge portion of the population who will retire broke or never experience retiring and having *a life*. Can you imagine yourself truly having to continue working for the rest of your life? With my latest company, CRN (Consumer Resources Network), I came up with a formula I call the *2-5 PLAN to Financial Freedom*. It is utilizing the best information on the laws and principles of this universe, resources, and support systems available out there to help members and consumers. By applying the secrets of the wealthy, utilizing OPM (this also means banks' monies), OPT, OPE and through the MSI (multiple sources of income concepts), anyone can realize his or her dreams and visions, reach his or her fullest financial potential. I am currently working on my next book that can better explain how this 2-5 plan works. Remember, even the most known, wealthiest people in America and around the world do not only have one business or source of income. They diversify, network, or have multiple sources.

Let me share with you here one of my greatest discoveries. This is significant to our subject matter and we can refer to this as *The Power of Duplication and Multiplication*. This amazing simple formula works whether you are counting people or money. Let's take an example in a form of a million dollar question:

Which will you take now, a hundred thousand dollars or a dollar multiplying itself every day for the next 30 days? Most people by impulse will take the hundred thousand dollars. Few who will take time to do the math may decide otherwise. Examine this:

1. $1.
2. $2.
3. $4.
4. $8.
5. $16.
6. $32.
7. $64
8. $128.
9. $256.
10. $512.
11. $1,024.
12. $2,048
13. $4,096.
14. $8,192.
15. $16,384.
16. $32,768.
17. $65,536.
18. $131,072.
19. $262,144.
20. $524,288.
21. $1,048,576.
22. $2,097,152.
23. $4,194,304.
24. $8,388,608.
25. $16,777,216.
26. $33,554,432.
27. $67,108,864.
28. $134,217,728.
29. $268,435,456.
30. $536,870,912.

Incredible! Even just a 1% result from this effort is over 5 Million!!!

What about *Network Marketing*? A good number of the upper ten percent of our population derives its wealth from this great business concept, as briefly mentioned earlier. Network marketing strategies of different companies come in various forms. This can be a good way to establish multiple sources of income (MSI) if allowable. This method can be so affordable and possible for any average and ordinary person to be in business, even part time or spare time. You can even work from the comfort of your home in your pajamas. Imagine that. The process is simple. It involves sharing, connecting, or team working with others to accomplish a common goal. It is nothing new, even as old as the first business ever created, since without connecting or working with people and other businesses, how can you see any business survive? Like any other type of business, a few networking ones went sour and caused alarm to some people. As a result, some people who may have heard of such may feel very cautious when approached. To consider one, you have to really check the background of the company, the management, recommendations, etc. They should have legitimate products or services and should not cost you any amount that you feel will cause you to be devastated if it doesn't work out. But your goal is definitely that you will make it work! And as long as you will and you find the right company to team with, you are in for so much *personal development, fun,* and *rewards,* not to mention a real time and experience of your life!

Success in life, even financial success, is not just all concepts, formulas, and figures. In fact it starts with the right *mindset*. An *open and ready mind*, a mind that made a *decision*, made a *commitment* by equipping itself with the knowledge and tools needed; one that is *prepared to take action* and *do what it will take* to get the job done, to accomplish a goal.

To summarize the FORMULA:
You **THINK** (see/plan in your mind) –> You **FEEL** (believe with passion, conviction with your heart) –> You **ACT your PLAN** (put into action) = **GREAT RESULT** (dreams/goals MANIFEST, become REALITY)

> *"Success is a predictable result"*
> Bob Proctor

> *"We become what we think about"*
> Earl Nightingale

Reading the daily local newspaper few years back, San Jose Mercury News, I was delighted to read that scientists on their extensive research of how unexplainable phenomena happen (like what people call *miracles*), found out and concluded that *when you believe on something, there are energy forces in this universe that brings together what you are thinking into a reality.* Beautiful! Isn't that amazing? Now, what are these *energy forces* in the universe they are talking about? Something we cannot see, right? Something we may never comprehend, but it is there. Could this life's phenomena be as simple as God telling us, *"Seek and you will find. Knock and it will be opened to you. Ask and it will be given to you"*? Like the wind blowing, we do not know where it is coming from, where it is going, but it is there for us to feel. The air that we breathe is vital to keep us alive. We cannot see the air, but it is always there for us to continue to live. Think it, believe it, and let the universe work it out for you.

> *"We make a living by what we get, but we make a life by what we give"*
>
> Sir Winston Churchill,
> British Prime Minister

> *"Whether you believe you can do a thing or believe you can't, you are right."*
>
> Henry Ford

Three Types of People

- Those who *make* things happen.
- Those who *watch* things happen.
- Those who *wonder* what happened.

Which one are you? Take note of any sports, games, movies, or shows. Only a few are actual players, a good number are watchers, and the majority are out there and are not aware or simply don't care of the happenings. I see some parallel on these: the approximately two percent who make things happen, the twenty-three percent who watch things happen (some with partial participation), and the seventy-five percent who have no clue what's happening or wonder what happened. Interestingly this is about the same as some familiar statistics by the Department of Labor: two percent financially independent (making things happen), twenty-three percent who watch and wait or procrastinate, and seventy-five percent who have no time or are too busy working or whatever, and/or always seem to complain about money. Almost all of us, at least once in our life, have fallen into any of these three categories, mostly the last two. Something to think about, the potential waste of valuable human resources we have. Each of us, as we choose to, can decide to move up or have an upgrade, don't you think? To be most productive and be able to contribute to the solutions, to the best quality of life for all of us, we each need to strive to *make* good things happen.

> *"Get all the education you can, but then, by God, do something. Don't just stand there; make it happen."*
>
> Lee Iococca,
> American business executive

> *"Don't' aim for success if you want it; just do what you love and believe in, and it will come naturally."*
>
> David Frost,
> English writer, journalist

Life will Give You What You will Take

So, what do you really want in life? What do you really want to do and accomplish? It does not matter how small or big it is. It could be as simple as going to the next block or as grand as going to the moon. Nothing is impossible! What you have in mind, what you have already established, pictured, and believed you can do, and it will happen. It is just a matter of time. Sure, you can start small. That is all right, then keep practicing, taking baby steps until you feel comfortable enough that YOU CAN DO IT! When you reach that point of development, when you begin to grasp "the power within you" that Tony Robbins and other famous speakers are talking about, then you are ready for bigger things, bigger goals and dreams. Is this really for everybody? The laws of this universe apply to all, are available to anyone, but again it is limiting beliefs that hinder people from unleashing the power within to make things happen. Life will give you what you will take. You can say, "Oh, I am happy with what I have," or "I believe there is really more for me in life. The dream I see, the goal I establish, can be a reality!" The universe will gladly respond to this, "*Then so be it!*"

If you found a genie in a bottle, and it asked you for three wishes, and whatever you wished for would be yours, what would be your three wishes? The only limitations you have are the limitations that you put in front of you. It is what you say because you think, you believe; your choice, your decision. It is *what you asked*, and therefore it *is given* to you.

Your dad (or your boss) can tell right away what you are thinking or believing when you approach him. He can tell if you can accept *yes* or *no*. Your level of confidence, conviction, attitude, positive or negative, reflected on your approach determines whether you are going to get what you are asking for. In a sense it is not actually your dad or your boss who gives you the bike or a raise. Believe it or not, it is *you*! Let me explain further. When you approach your dad or your boss, and you are saying, or your body language reflects that, "If you give it, great. If not, it is okay, maybe next time," your posture indicates to them that *you are not ready*! You are not convinced enough that you need it or deserve it. It is not that they don't want to give to you what you are asking for; you already indicated to them that you can still wait, so be it. But when you approach with full confidence and conviction that looks like you are not taking *no* for an answer, you are likely to get what you ask for. Why? Because you are sending a strong *vibration* that *you are ready* for it or *you deserve it!* (If that is really the case.) At that point the energy forces in the universe will arrange for things to happen to make that a reality. Your dad or your boss suddenly will say something like, "We can arrange that," or "I believe we can do something to make that happen." Isn't that amazing?

The problem with most people is they live their lives with *fear* of the unknown. This does not work; fear of what? Fear is also associated with avoiding risk or mistake or humiliation. You can clearly see the role of fear, right? Yes, it is something that you consciously or unconsciously keep putting in front of you to keep blocking you from taking the necessary steps for you to achieve what you really want. Think again about the number of opportunities you have missed because you let fear of the unknown stop you. Let us be very clear of this again, *fear is nothing but a device to hinder, block, or stop you.* You need to learn to *conquer* your fear, or it will continue to conquer you. You decide. My additional tip: besides my conscious decision that fear will not conquer me, what helped me most to conquer fear is the knowledge that the nature of God is goodness or love, not fear. I embrace His nature in me. If God is in me, then fear of the unknown has no place in me. The only fear that I know is the reverence that I have to the wonderful God who created and is in me.

Most successful people are known to be *risk takers* (calculated risks) who accept or embrace mistakes, which they consider stepping stones necessary to learn and grow in order succeed. How and when will you be successful if you don't give yourself those needed opportunities to learn and grow when you seem to be always trapped by something or somebody. Can you be one of these successful people? Yes, when you are ready to set yourself *free*!

> *"Keep away from people who try to belittle your ambitions. Small people always do that, but the really great make you feel that you, too, can become great."*
>
> Mark Twain

> *"Achieving goals by themselves will never make us happy in the long term: it's who you become, as you overcome the obstacles necessary to achieve your goals, that can give you the deeper sense and most long-lasting sense of fulfillment."*
>
> Tony Robbins

The Secrets to a Joyful and Meaningful Life

"If we did all the things we are capable of doing, we would truly astound ourselves."

- Thomas Edison,
American inventor

Life's ABCs

Recalling our ABCs is easy. More or less it will come out like this: *A* is for apple, *B* is for ball, *C* is for cat…something like that, right? Without making an effort, it is amazing how our marvelous memory bank (brain) automatically produces what we stored during our school days. Yes, we can easily recall our alphabet. Oh, thank God for our mothers and fathers, teachers and grandparents, and anybody else who unselfishly gave up so much of their valuable time so that we could begin to learn how to read and write. Otherwise our society would brand us as illiterate, and we would be told we have no future.

I admit that I used to share the same misconception that if you do not know how to read and write, it is almost impossible to survive in this competitive world, much less succeed. Well, I will not hesitate to admit that I was dead wrong on this one. Over the years I have found that there are lots of people who, for various reasons, did not have the opportunity to learn the alphabet or go to school, who have no or very limited scholastic abilities, and yet they became very successful in life. I ask, how is that possible?

Now wait a minute. Let's recall our classmates who were excellent in reading and writing composition or those who were very scholastic. How successful are they now? Apparently mastering our school ABCs and other subjects was not enough to guarantee us success in life. And what's more, many who never learned school basics have succeeded anyway in spite of their lack of formal education. How did they do it? This amazes me. Are we missing something here? Education is considered very costly. Yet we seek and sacrifice a lot to be educated, because it will pay off, of course. Does it always? Nowadays we are seeing graduates who are more burdened with mounting debts than they are excited of the careers they are getting into. They have spent so much money and worked so hard to prepare for "their future." It was too long ago, and I didn't know the name of the speaker whose comment I could never forget. He was saying that our schools are so good in teaching our students technical know-hows to prepare them for future careers but have failed to prepare them for real life. Interestingly I noted several people nodding their heads in agreement when this was stated. Are schools' roles really just confined to preparing our children for future careers? Well, who's going to prepare them; who is responsible in preparing them for life successes?

Perhaps we need to evaluate what we learned from our schools, what *education* and *knowledge* really mean. If you are seriously seeking the answer, let me share with you what I have learned over the years from watching, listening, talking, and reading about successful, healthy, and happy people. They are glad to share their secrets with anybody. Their secrets, though they will say "are no secrets," are that they learned and practiced *life's basic learning*, which I condensed in ABC format, meaning the basics of life, how to live it, and what is truly needed to learn and develop if we are to be successful in facing real life, challenging situations.

Except for the few words or concepts, most of what you will discover about life's ABCs are familiar. Some you may already be practicing. Some you may find still an adventure to be learned. I also found out that it is never too late for anyone to learn. As you begin to practice each one of these, you will find new meaning to life. Here are the *ABCs of Life*.

A – Attitude – Yes! The first thing we need to develop is the right attitude, a good, positive outlook about anything and anybody. How do you see things? How do you react to situations? Having the right attitude is the ability to turn negatives into positives, to change unproductive thoughts to productive ones, to see and remember the good and beautiful things about a person or situation instead of the opposite. If you have the right attitude, you are already halfway there.

Appreciation – This goes hand in hand with the right attitude. It is being appreciative, grateful, or thankful for what you have, for things and people around you, for the God who gives you each day of your life.

B – Believe – Yes! Learn to believe! Have faith in yourself and others. Believe that good things can happen and that anything is possible if you believe enough. The more that you can expand your horizon of belief, the better you will be. When you believe in something (a cause, a program) or somebody (God, yourself, others), it automatically opens the door for an opportunity or a more meaningful relationship. Believing breaks the barriers; it bridges the gap. Try it!

C – Commitment – Honor the promises you have made to yourself and others. It takes commitment for any relationship to work, for the task to be accomplished, and for each of us to make this world a better place in which to live.

Courage – it takes courage to make a commitment, to stand for something, to follow through on what you have promised. It takes courage to start something new, to adapt to changes, to face many challenges. Courage is what creates our heroes.

Communication – Keep your communication *open*. Learn to talk and listen. Say what you mean and mean what you say.

Consideration – It takes careful thought not to hurt or inconvenience others.

Care and *Compassion* – Showing or giving affection, being thoughtful, showing mercy. Mother Teresa, our doctors, nurses, caregivers, firefighters, and volunteers are great examples.

D – Dream/Vision – The ability to see what your mind can conceive and hold onto it until it is achieved. Believe in your dreams. They can happen.

Decision/Destination – Accomplishment starts from a decision. Have a sense of direction; know where you are going. Your decision brings up the road map leading to your chosen destination.

Determination – Your ability to persist, to keep on, to not give up or quit. You know you will meet obstacles, but nothing will or can stop you.

Discipline – Develop self-guidance and self-motivation; be more responsible for your actions.

Do it! – Take action. As you do it, give only your best. Remember to do to others what you want others to do to you.

E – Enthusiasm – Learn to live with excitement and energy from within.

Environment – Each of us needs to strive to preserve our environment for us and for our next generation. Our environment is not just the trees, the ocean, the air, or the endangered species. It is also *us, the people*. You and I need to work together to focus and help preserve the best quality of life for everybody to share.

Empathy – Understanding other people better by putting yourself in someone else's shoes or position.

F – Focus – Concentrate and don't lose sight of your goals and dreams. Do not get distracted. Keep your eyes focused on the target.

Family – The central unit of our society, which we should all strive to preserve.

Flexibility – The ability to adjust or to adapt to changes when new situations arise. This is one trait or skill that when developed can tremendously help you in every area of your life.

Forgiveness – To cease from feeling angry, bitter, or resentful, to heal oneself as well as others.

G – Goal – Establish your short- and long-term goals, what you wish to accomplish. Do what is needed and stick to it.

Generosity – Giving principle: "It is when you give that you receive."

This is a good start. Why not try producing words that come to mind for H – Z? Sure you can. If you do, will you share them also? In my upcoming book, *Life's ABCs*, the rest of the letters up to Z will be discussed in more detail, along with how they relate and empower you to fulfill your dreams and purpose in life.

Positive words and actions produce POSITIVE RESULTS. These positive results in turn produce a chain of positive effects that lead to a better quality of life for everyone.

Negative words and actions, in contrast, produce negative results. Negative and vulgar words should be eliminated from our daily vocabularies simply because these words have nothing good to bring to us. Positive words are called positive because the effect adds to life. The negative words only reduce, minimize, and undermine. More and more people are carelessly using these undesirable words without realizing the immediate and lasting negative effect or damage these words are creating. They hurt, demean, and dehumanize an individual or group. Quick, short, casually used words that can create a negative effect, sometimes even devastating effects, on people and our surroundings should be avoided. A reader of the review copy of this book had an interesting comment: "The overuse of curse words and how many have become desensitized to them… But they really are ugly and people just don't realize it, because they think they're 'cool,' especially young people."

Start using and encouraging others to use the ABCs of life. We need to be careful of the words we use. You've probably heard of this already, "Your word declares the outcome." I refer to the topic of Life's ABCs as *the power of expressed and written words*. The words you use can manifest and can be a reality.

> "The greatest revolution of our generation
> is the discovery that human beings, by
> changing the inner attitudes of their minds
> can change the outer aspects of their lives."
>
> William James, American psychologist
> and philosopher

Learn to Live with a Song

Can you imagine what our world would be like without music, without a song to sing or to listen to? It would be a very dull world indeed!

Music is the art and science of combining the sounds of voices or instruments or both in a pleasing sequence or combination. It can be any pleasant sound or series of sounds, such as a bird song or the sound of flowing water, which is often referred to as music to the soul. A *song* is a musical composition for singing.

We listen to music just about everywhere we go, practically every day. Without much realization of it, we can appreciate what music does for us. Music is a big part of our lives simply because of the *way it affects us.* Each of us has a favorite song that we love to listen to. And anyone can sing along, not just gifted singers. Each one of us can sing! There are songs that can change our mood, make us cry, make us remember important events or people. Music is amazingly powerful in moving people to take action or experience certain feelings. Have you ever noticed how music and songs are carefully selected in movies to fit particular scenes? There are songs that encourage people to exercise (physical); that stimulate romantic feelings or other emotions (emotional); motivate a person to use his mental power and be more productive (mental); feel closer to or be in the presence of God, especially in a church setting (spiritual); appreciate the meaning of friendship and humanity (social), etc. That is why records and mp3s sell so well; because they appeal to our whole being. They help make our world more beautiful and more colorful.

Because of our individuality, there will always be differences in our personal preferences of music, and we should respect one another for that. However, be aware that there is also so-called music that is more of a peculiar noise. The creator may be expressing anger, hatred, frustration, or even desperation, which can readily be transmitted to and internalized by the unsuspecting listener. There is no telling of the effect it can have on that listener. If the listener cannot detach him or herself from the message of that peculiar sound, the result can be very dangerous. We can prevent further undesirable events by alerting parents, educators, and responsible regulators to be aware and make effort to orient our children about the *psychological process* involved here.

Instead, let us create good music in our hearts. Be selective by listening to music and singers that express or reflect happiness, love, peace, and friendship. Carry a good song to live by. Like a refreshing water or a fresh breeze, a good song or soothing music brings healing, inspiration, encouragement, peace, reconciliation, team spirit, hope, and amazing power to go on. Singing while working or driving creates wonders.

Do you have a song in your heart? Get a good one and keep singing it. You will be amazed how it pleasantly wakes you up in the morning so you can start a wonderful day.

Learn to Live with a Motto

"Love conquers all" is a short phrase but remains as one of the greatest mottos ever. A motto like this one does not need much explanation. It pretty much explains the power in itself.

A *motto* is a short sentence or phrase adopted as a rule of conduct or as expressing the aims and ideals of an individual, a family, a group, a country, or an institution. Simple, short phrases similar to the one above have influenced and inspired people for ages.

Mottos are widely used, and we are familiar with many of them. Our early government adopted one and even inscribed it on our currencies, *"In God we trust."* Families, friends, teams, and different groups share this motto, *"United we stand, divided we fall."* A school has this written on its wall, *"Knowledge is a terrible thing to waste."* Hospitals may have this one as their motto, *"Patients first."* Stores and businesses have mottos like this: *"Customer first," "Customer satisfaction is our #1 policy."* In sports you can frequently hear this one, *"The game is not over until it is over."* Regardless of your involvement or interest, each of us can learn from mottos.

Probably the most widely used motto in sports and also for business is "Just DO IT!" A known sport merchandiser took it as their slogan and made "Just do it!" a household phrase and, together with known celebrities, helped Nike reach phenomenal growth and popularity. Mottos and phrases like these can be very powerful. When you hear a parent, a boss, or a leader say, "Don't just think about it or say it, DO IT!" it seems enough to actually influence people to take action or do something.

Can you see how this powerful concept can be used to influence us individually and collectively? We can use it to adopt something we like, which will help us grow and improve. We can even make up our own motto(s) to live by.

In my case, mottos are a natural part of my life. We use mottos a lot at home and at school. My personal mottos were mostly passed on by my father (though I never really tracked down where he got them or where they came from). Others I picked up from school and from other people. The mottos will most likely be passed onto my children as well. Let me share my favorites with you.

"Do to others what you want others to do to you." Don't do to others what you don't want others do to you." This reminds me always to put myself in the other person's place and think, *"How I want to be treated is the way I should also treat this person."* Of course, I still goof once in a while, but I try my best and learn more from each incident. Overall

this motto has helped me a lot when dealing with others, including my dear husband and children.

"Do it right, or don't do it at all." That means give your best at all times, or don't even bother if you cannot give your best. It also means do it if you know it is the right thing to do. If not, if you are in doubt, don't do it at all. Strong words from my father, but I like it. It makes a lot of sense to me.

"Say what you mean, and mean what you say. Otherwise, why say it?" Is a very impressive phrase I got from a very remarkable lady, my Aunt Letty.

"Don't do tomorrow what you can do today." Put even more simply, do not procrastinate. There are times when I relax and take it easy, thinking it will not hurt to postpone something, that I really need the break or to rest. Otherwise, if I can do it now, why waste my time? Time is so valuable. It is one thing I cannot take back once it has passed. Utilizing my time wisely makes me more productive and useful. That adds to my feeling of fulfillment and happiness, of course. This motto reminds me each day to do as much as I can for the day. This is also where I learned to have a sense of urgency, to treat each of my day as if it is my last, so I ought to give my best each day.

"When one door closes, a better one is waiting for me." This is a great motto that will prevent us from being very disappointed or depressed when things didn't work out as we wanted to. Giving up will never be an option in order to survive tough times in life, because this motto will remind us that there are always brighter tomorrows, better opportunities.

Mottos have been a treasured guide for people to living a more fruitful, meaningful life. It is like adding another valuable tool to your "backpack for living a good life in harmony with your universe."

America, there must have been a good reason for our forefathers to have chosen a motto for our country. We should not lose sight of it and always remember what made AMERICA a very special and strong nation. It is a short motto but a very powerful and meaningful one, "IN GOD WE TRUST."

Morals and Family Values are Vital

Is this subject even still relevant? For humankind's sake, if we still really value our quality of life, then it is relevant. What is happening in our world today, probably even in our own neighborhoods, is alarming. There is a loud cry for help, for solutions. Should we say, "Let's go re-discover these morals and family values, for they may be the only hope for our society and for our children?" If we say *yes*, then let's move ahead.

This led me to open my dictionary to find out what is the definition of *morals* and *values*. On *morals* my dictionary says, "Of or concerned with the goodness and badness of human character or with the principles of what is right and wrong in conduct; capable of understanding and living by the rules of morality." On *"values,"* it says, "Standards or principles considered valuable or important in life." The presented meanings are simple and self-explanatory, indicative of their relevance in our life.

Next, I went to the library and a bookstore. Mission: "Search for missing morals and values." I could not help but wonder how many other people out there are doing the same. I found it interesting that there were stacks and stacks of books about computers, success, self-improvement, physical fitness, and how to look good, money matters, cookbooks, all kinds of subjects, including those that I believe should not even be in our libraries in the first place, but I found close to nothing about morals and family values. No wonder we are missing out. If it is so important, vital to our life, how come there is such a scarcity of resources to gain further knowledge about these subjects? I am curious. For so many years that our children spend in schools from their early childhood, are these subjects even included or incorporated in what they are learning? It is very critical that we answer these questions if we care enough for the present and future generations. Comparing it to the importance of bottled water to most people nowadays, it is like there was an embargo on bottled water and now it is rarely available. Naturally people were dying of thirst, so they resorted to drinking even polluted water. Get the picture?

Whose fault is it? Those who think they are smart enough and have no need for morals and family values? Is it the average and ordinary folks who once again gave in to the great old liar of this world? Is it the merchants who introduced all these latest, modern gadgets that seem like we cannot live without, that make us forget what is really more important in our lives? WAKE UP! We all need self check-ups. Obviously we all must take individual responsibility. We are probably realizing now that no amount of riches, great technology, not even education, modern science, and psychology can give us morals and values. It begins from the heart and soul of each individual. What do we choose to think and feel inside? What do you believe?

So where do we and our children learn morals and family values? Shouldn't we learn them from *home, school, church,* and *everywhere* else possible? You know the answer to that. Success and victory in life can be better accomplished by those standing on solid ground.

> *"In the course of history, there comes a time when humanity is called to shift to a new level of consciousness, to reach a higher moral ground. A time when we have to shed our fear and give hope to each other… That time is now."*
>
> Dr. Wangari Maathari, Nobel Prize winner, environmental and political activist

What about PRAYER?

When people pray, they believe. And because they believe, *miracles* happen. Amazing things happen that are hard to explain and so there are people who do not believe because they said there is no scientific basis. Does it has to be scientific for someone to believe? Isn't science created by men also, to try to explain things? For me, it is just simple common sense that if science or any of us, as a matter of fact, can easily explain how miracles happen, then people believe as it turns to be an accepted concept, law, or principle. Then there will no longer be, as it will no longer be called, miracle. Miracle is very interesting for me because it clearly shows human limitations; when supposedly to humans are "impossible become possible." In spite of mankind's advancement including computers, satellites, etc., it is fascinating to note that when it comes to Mother Nature, it's so difficult for men to accurately predict forceful or unpredictable weather, earthquakes and such; much more do anything to prevent it. To this point, we are still at nature's mercy or fury, and there's possibly not much that we can do but PRAY! I found an interesting article few years back that says there was a group of scientist who made a study on how miracles happen. They discovered that there are *energy forces* in this universe that bring together what we believe into reality. That did not surprise me at all. It just reaffirmed what I already knew. In short, something good happens when we pray and believe. So, why stop the flow of good blessings?

Someone who cares gave me the advice that if I want to sell the book, it will be best not to mention things about God or even prayer. I appreciate such concern, but if I were to follow his advice, there would be no book at all. This is not about religious belief. I am but a well-being advocate. Our government, some schools, and even some homes have stayed away from what they refer as an "issue you do not want to touch." The problems and tragedies happening in our schools today eventually brought concern to parents, school officials, and nation's leaders alike. It is time to examine, evaluate what and where we went wrong. What can be done? I, in particular, while gripped with sadness watching the news, thought how it became a national tragedy for schools to stay away from prayers and blocked students from finding meaningful relationship with God, the very source of our existence. It does not matter what people call their Supreme God or how they practice their belief. It remains that we all have basic spiritual needs that need to be met. Has it occurred to us that we call our *fathers* in different ways, such as Papa, Dad, Pops, Tata, Tatay, and probably a hundred more other names around the world? Why shy away from the one who magnificently created us all? I have not found anyone yet who truly believes that he or she came from a big bang, a microorganism, an animal origin, or whatever else. Do you? Those are theories far from truth, a smart distraction. No matter what, that bang, microorganism, or animal still came from somewhere or someone who created it, right? It is because only God is the true beginning and end. More and more scientists now are willing to admit that on their futile efforts to discredit God, they found God.

One day I asked my youngest daughter her opinion about prayers at school and other public places. The reply was, "Mom, you know I want prayers at the school, everywhere, but they don't do it because of others' religious beliefs." That seems to be a harmless reason to show respect for others. Doesn't it? I cannot help but remember that at the hospital there were few incidents when someone refused to receive a blood transfusion because of religious belief. But the hospital did not ban the blood transfusion because of that, did they? This *life-saving necessity* is continuously made *available to everyone* unless they refuse to receive it, which is their right. The proportion of those who have received and been saved by blood transfusion is far greater than those who refused it. They could have been all dead if the hospital had decided to ban blood transfusions out of respect for others' beliefs. Yes, religious beliefs are definitely each individual's right, but these are totally different from having an opportunity to commune and build a relationship with God, which we all *need*.

Who does not need prayer to commune with God? Can your physical body last without food? What will happen to your mind if it is never stimulated or fed with good thoughts? What happens to an individual who never feels love or acceptance or is banned from feeling or expressing emotions? Can you survive long without working and no money in your pocket? What would it be like for a person to be isolated on an island all by himself? If your spirit is the driving force in your life, shouldn't its need be met as well? Think about it.

Sure, parents and children even at home have different food preferences and eating habits. But in spite of all these differences, it is not a problem. Since food and water are basic necessities, preference is not an issue. Children can amazingly discuss these different practices and preferences with much interest without getting into a fight about them. Let us look at our school settings, especially our public schools. Educators are not the issue here. They are wonderful and greatly appreciated for working so hard to teach our children. The true issue is that someone or something has managed to infiltrate our school system to accomplish its own goal, to remove the means for our children to openly practice meaningful relationship with God and to develop the spirit with good morals and values. As a result, it should not surprise anyone at all that unthinkable things are now happening in our schools. Common ground rules of respect can be laid out for the different religious practices, but a few minutes or quiet time is surely needed by these children if we want them to grow as *calm, composed, more complete, fulfilled individuals*. We just cannot deny them of that need.

I can see no harm for students or children to believe in God. On the contrary, amazing things happen as evidenced by the life of a very bright student, Karen Cheng. Her name and picture was featured on the front page of a local newspaper in March 1996 saying, "Star student passes for being the best." She was declared as possibly the brightest high-school student in the nation, being a straight-A student with a perfect score on both the Scholastic Achievement Tests and the University of California acceptance index. Nobody had ever scored perfect on both before. I met with her, congratulated her, and asked if she could review my manuscript. She accepted. Her inputs to my first book, *Today's S.O.S.*, were valuable because her comments were not only intelligent but meaningful. It may interest you that her main comment was, "I was interested to find that the book deals with God also. Bring in God throughout the book, because God fills every part of a believer's life." That is not only intelligent, that is wisdom! Again, this is not about the religion or being religious. It is the *personal relationship with God* that makes a person complete, a big difference in one's life. Do we really want our children to be successful in all aspects of their lives? Simply take the formula from Karen. It works!

Do we really want the best for our children? Do we want a more positive change in our society and a better harmony in our environment? It is not just our children at school or the students at colleges and universities who need to connect with someone bigger and better than them, but *we all do*. Our parents, teachers, health workers, leaders in our churches, schools, communities, and government all need prayers as we face the demands of our daily responsibilities wherever we are. With the problems we already have in our society, may these old phrases be a good reminder:

The fear (reverence) of the Lord is the beginning of wisdom.

The family that prays together stays together.

Now, What's Next?

For this is not the end, but just the beginning.

The Key is Within You

Time is gold. Health is wealth. Knowledge is treasure.

You see how the tens of thousand of dollars that I spent to buy all the books and tapes, to attend the camps, and all these expensive seminars paid off for me? My husband used to say, "Are you crazy, spending all these money for what? You could be buying other important *things*." For me, he is referring to things that don't last or depreciate in value instead of appreciating. Now he understands and agrees with me. It is what you call investment. And the best investment we can make is to *invest in ourselves* first in order to gain more knowledge and personal development. When you know that *you know*, you gain more confidence. That confidence allows you to be more comfortable to make decisions. That decision will spring you into action, which brings you closer to your vision or the things you really want to do and achieve in life. Focus not just on financial, but consider your total well being.

There is a fine line between winning and losing. It is your choice, your decision. It is what you focus on, what you want to be.

Losing	Winning
It's not possible; I quit	I believe
I can't	I can
I may; I'll see if…	I will
Do nothing	Press on; Make it happen

Damaging, Unhealthy Emotions/Feelings: Hate, fear, worry, greed, jealousy, unforgiving, resentment, bitterness, burned out.

Living, Healthy Emotions/Feelings: Love, joy, peace, understanding, giving, forgiving.

All these are considered normal emotions, something that naturally come to each human being as a sudden feeling, a spurt of the moment. What you do after that few seconds or minutes is what matters. For the living emotions, you may hold onto them as long as you want because they are healthy to your whole being. You have to be more aware of the damaging emotions as they come because they are dangerous to your total health and well being, like cancer cells. These need to be put in control as soon as you recognize they are coming to you. Shake them off. Take some deep breaths. Switch back to the living emotions as soon as possible.

Disabling/Damaging Words and Thoughts: Cursing, profanity, words that should not be expressed and cannot be written in this book.

Power Living Words and Thoughts: Wonderful! Amazing! Awesome! Beautiful! Marvelous! Terrific! Fantastic! Fabulous! Super! Great! Love, joy, faith, believe, peace, hope, abundance are sample of positive and powerful words. If what you are expressing is a living word (healing, healthy), GO SAY IT! *"I love you." "I forgive you." "You can do it!" "You're a superstar!" "I believe in you."* These are the thoughts that should fill your mind more and what should be spoken more to others, especially to children. It will make a huge difference to you and everyone around you.

People waste more time and energy thinking about why something can't work, can't be done, or why it can't happen. Rather, think of how it can work and how you can make it happen. The thing is, if something has to happen, it will happen with or without you. *"If it is to be, it's up to me."* If something has to change for the better, it will be up to YOU.

YOU can be TRANSFORMED if you want to. It's your decision…

From:			
Wonderer	→ Spectator	→	Active Participant/Maker
Loser	→ Mediocre	→	Winner
Borrower	→ Owner	→	Investor/Multiplier
Poor	→ Middle Class	→	Wealthy/Abundant
Dependent/Taker	→ Self sufficient	→	Financially Independent/Giver
Nobody	→ Average and Ordinary	→	Extraordinary

In the Book of Life, you will find that many supposedly hopeless people in history were transformed because of faith or belief: a blind from birth gained sight; a bleeding woman healed; a lame walked; a captive freed.

It is not what other people think or what your horoscope says about you. The secret is in what *you think* and *believe*. The ultimate secret is YOU, in relation to *the One who lovingly created you*. You now just entered a new beginning, facing an unlimited universe, and everything in it is at your disposal for good reasons and purpose, for you to enjoy and to share with the world. Go ahead. Create your dream board. Write down *"My Personal Dreams, Goals, Mission, and Purpose,"* whatever applies. Focus on these each day when you wake up. You may put it on your refrigerator or your favorite mirror or anywhere visible to you. Be specific. Put a target date. All you need now is to believe and take action or act on your belief. Walk each day, carrying the faith in your heart. Go and make great things happen! Watch the sleeping giant in you wake up to the realization that you are meant to be a conqueror, finding your true treasures. Live and enjoy your life to the fullest, for the delight and honor of your Creator, your God, your Father.

The key to success in life, healthy, joyful, wealthy, or abundant living is already *in* you. *Today* is the time and the chance you have been waiting for. Don't let anything or anybody stop you now. GO FOR IT! Follow your dreams. The key to life success and victory is *within* you. Welcome home!

Summary:

- *Believe.* The universe is more than happy to give you what you want – your dreams, your visions, your goals, your strong desires in life. You and the universe can only harmoniously make things happen when you are *open*, meaning you *believe* that whatever good things that come to your mind are real. Use your imagination as if it is already there and you are simply taking the *action* (moved by your belief), which is necessary to make things happen. Again, when you believe, you spring into action. That action brings you together with the people and events set up by the universe toward your path as a result of the harmony or connection you created with your belief. When you are closed or do not believe or have stopped believing, that immediately shuts off the flow of what the universe can help you accomplish. Remember, if what you are thinking is something good, it is just a matter of *yes* or *wait*. It is only *no* when you stop believing or if the outcome will not be good for you. Of course, the universe will not stop you when you insist your way anyway. Just know that there are corresponding consequences to your actions. Predictable results: you already know that what you expect/believe is what will happen. Guard your mind of what you believe, because that is what will happen.

- *Be of courage.* There is a good and evil side on each story, book, play, or movie. The villains are real in our true life. The universe is designed or created for the good, for our good. The evil thoughts, desires, and results only lead to loss, violent death, or destruction brought by the people influenced by or who allowed themselves to be subjected to the evil doings. Once you realize and made a decision that that is not what you want in your life, believe that you have the power in you to resist the evil, to decline or reject the destructive suggestions. You will learn to discern, the ability to distinguish from right or wrong, from good or evil thoughts, feelings or actions. This is where we truly need God in us, the good spirit in us, His Spirit in you, because in time of human weakness, He can make us strong, victorious. What do you believe?

- *Think BIG.* It does not matter what your dream or goal is, big or small, when you believe, it will happen, and that is exactly what you will get. So, if the dream that came to you seems to be huge or impossible, believe it anyway and *go for it*! Remember, it is not called a miracle if it is easy to achieve. It is called so because it is supposed to be impossible. So, what do you have to lose? Dream BIG! Believe! And Go for it!

- *Take ACTION.* Did you listen to Mark and Earl's message? If you did, great job! If not, or you haven't heard of it ever, do yourself a big favor, go in front of your computer and listen. If you really want to achieve something great for yourself, you've got to *take action*! Gaining information alone is not good enough. Knowledge alone without the application or action results in nothing. You have to develop the habit of actually putting the knowledge or gathered information into ACTION. Action creates RESULT. Good, constructive action produces productive *reaction* or *results* (applying the *cause and effect principle*). You need to translate your beliefs into action. Make things happen. You, too, can be a *mountain mover*, an *impossibility achiever*!

- *Multiply.* You are meant to be fruitful, productive, to grow and multiply, become an extension of God's blessings to others. Like a seed that is meant to be planted and nurtured so it can produce fruits. Then you have something to share for others to enjoy. Just like the leading character in a great movie that, against all odds and adversities, at the end will come out triumphant and victorious, bringing not only great entertainment to the viewers but most likely a great inspiration to many who needed just that boost to help them go on in life, to dream and believe again. To believe one more time that he, too, can do it. It can happen to him, too. As you exercise this principle, the more you will appreciate the concept, *the power of duplication and multiplication.*

- *Give.* "It is when you give that you receive, and the more you give the more you will receive." This does not only apply to money. You can give or share time, talent, ability, skill, and other resources. There is no small or insignificant piece in the game of completing the puzzle. Giving is like *planting seeds*. We can only expect a good harvest or result when we plant good seeds, our contribution to this great universe of ours. It is an amazing miracle that one small seed, like a mustard, a corn, an orange, or so forth, which are too small or seem insignificant, can grow to huge plants or giant trees when planted and nurtured (given faith). These then provide great produce, beauty, shade, home to birds, etc., enough to help create and contribute to our beautiful world. Let us give, contribute our part. Find your seeds, plant them, nurture them, and we will gladly watch with you as you make them flourish and be productive.

- *Be happy, rejoicing always!* Be positive. Have fun. Laugh. We are in this big world together, and whether we like it or not, we will affect one another. We might as well *work together* for common good, for everybody's sake. Shall we? My husband and children occasionally remind me, "Mom, when you're not happy, we're not happy. When you are happy, we're all happy." Take notice of how the people around you at home, work, or anywhere else are when you are happy or grouchy. They are but reacting or responding to the vibration you are sending. (Remember the mirror?) As the old saying goes, *"Smile, and the world will smile back at you."*

Find a reason to be happy always. When you are *happy,* you bring *health* to yourself. When you are *healthy,* this makes *you appreciative and happy,* a cycle that will keep revolving in your life if you determine to do so. The best part is at that state that you become more of *a magnet* to good things in life (law of attraction). Learn to reject unhappy thoughts and suggestions; it's unhealthy, nonproductive.

Even the Book of Life talks clearly about this subject. *"Don't worry about anything. Instead pray for everything." "Rejoice always!"* The popular movie *The Lion King* has that message in spite of all difficulties and challenges, "Hakuna Matata," don't worry, be HAPPY!!!

You made it this far. You deserve the best ever bonus treasure:

Go to *www.markvictorhansen.com* and listen to a wonderful, powerful message from *Mark Victor Hansen* (*Chicken Soup for the Soul* and *One Minute Millionaire*) and respected legend *Earl Nightingale's "The Strangest Secret."* Be prepared to take notes. You can listen to it over and over again. You will discover your greatest treasure! Your life will never be the same again.

> *"Action is the antidote to despair."*
> Joan Baez, American folk singer

> *"One of the greatest of all principles is that men can do what they think they can do."*
> Norman Vincent Peale

At this point I want to make sure you picked up the seven golden seeds spread out in this book. Although there are more secrets revealed, the major ones that can significantly impact your life are on this checklist. Of course these secrets are nothing new and simply accumulation of information that has been available out there for all of us. Make sure you grasped or gained from them to be able to apply and enjoy their fruits. (If not, or still missing some, simply go back and pick up the rest). Here we go:

- The Power of God's Love in Us
- The Power Within You
- The Power of Believing, of Faith that Can Move Mountains
- The Law of Attraction
- The Power of Expressed and Written Words
- The Power of Duplication and Multiplication
- The Power of "WE" – Together Making A Difference

"Until you have learned to be tolerant with those who do not always agree with you; until you have cultivated the habit of saying some kind word of those whom you do not admire; until you have formed the habit of looking for the good instead of the bad there is in others, you will be neither successful nor happy."

Napoleon Hill

"Whoever renders service to many puts himself in line for greatness – great wealth, great return, great satisfaction, great reputation, and great joy."

Jim Rohn, entrepreneur, author, speaker

Now, What's Next?

A Shared Vision

I have said to myself several times, "If I can only finish this book, I will die fulfilled." Now that it is about finished and I am still alive, it only means that my purpose is not done yet, that there are still more things to be done. It has been the purpose of this book to reach others and to help them gain awareness, gain hope, and courage to go on, to move on with a better perspective or outlook in life. I believe that *each person*, even the person who seems hopeless, has *something good inside* of him or her. There are still talents, potentials, and valuable resources that remain untapped. It is my sincere belief that if even just one or two people may be touched or helped by this book, it will be all worth it.

In my vision I can see that I still have to go out and actively share the content of the book or else it will be just another book on the shelf collecting dust. I am happy to continue conducting seminars and organizing events, not just to promote the book, but to explain details and to answer questions. As I go around in the community on a daily basis, I see or meet homeless people with young children lining up at a homeless shelter or food pantry, veterans on the streets begging for help or work, and looks of distress or expression of desperation on more and more people. I feel the urgency of need for us to take action, to find immediate solutions to meet the people's needs in every area of their lives. With my very limited resources also, I know that the best I can do as my share is to put in words the facts, the realities, and the individual and collective proposed solutions.

We may not be able to solve all our problems. I would be lying to you if I did not admit that if things don't change (if we do not do our part to make the change), the possibility of our society totally deteriorating and our world headed for worse is great. This is a *wake-up call*. Do not confine your vision to yourself alone. Look around you. Remove those blindfolds, see and know what is truly going on. We are the true reality show. Be assured that as people gain knowledge on how to live and survive; acknowledge their spiritual need for themselves and for tough times like this that America and the world face; and learn to *care* and *live* again; whatever comes can be tackled. Those adversities should not rob us of the HOPE and the JOY that we deserve and can truly have.

I found out that I am not alone in my vision, that it is being shared in various ways by many. The vision of *equal opportunity* and *abundance for all* citizens was shared by our American forefathers. Abraham Lincoln and Martin Luther King Jr. are just two of many great people who shared the same vision for all the people in America. Today I am seeing that those dreams have not died. Their descendants, our generation, both men and women and even our youth still share the same dreams. It is just a matter of each of us doing our part in making those dreams a reality.

As I get more involved with communities, as I read the newspapers and listen to the television about sad events and stories, it is equally heartwarming and inspiring to hear individual efforts, different organizations' community programs, and team efforts. *People are reaching out to others.* We all hope that the government can help, but people are not just sitting around and waiting anymore. We know that our government does not have all the answers to everything, and it needs our help, too. So, people are now beginning to ask, *"What can I do?"* Or they are saying, *"I want to help; just let me know how."*

I believe that someday more and more people will find true happiness, better health, and peace of mind. There will be opportunities for them to express their talents and be their best; more dreams will be realized; and finally, people will experience more victories in their lives.

> *"The most powerful thing you can do to change the world, is to change your own beliefs about the nature of life, people, reality, to something more positive."*
>
> Shakti Gawain, personal development best-selling author.

Now, What's Next?

Together Making a Difference

*"In helping others, we shall help ourselves,
for whatever good we give out completes
the circle and comes back to us."*

Flora Edwards, author, writer

The situation we now face as a society can be summarized into four thoughts:
1. We have lost track of the real *values* in life, including moral and family values. We need to go back to our basic character molding for wellness.
2. We focus more on the cure (of health problems, what to do with the sick, the criminals, the homeless, etc.) instead of putting more attention on *prevention*.
3. We have become total strangers, not trusting or even knowing our own neighbors. We need to *get back to one another*, get to know one another, share our concerns and ideas.
4. We are so disintegrated; everyone is "doing their own thing." To find effective solutions, we need to learn to *work together*, cooperate, collaborate, support each other for a healthier community. We do not need disasters or calamities to find ourselves needing one another, helping one another. *Working together can be our way of life.*

We can RECOVER! We can REBOUND! We can REBUILD! My vision shows people realizing that going back to basics is the only way to build a solid foundation for ourselves and for our society. To build a solid, strong, steady, and stable foundation applies to an individual, a marriage, a family, a team, a community, and a society. Just like building a house, it does not matter how big or fancy the house is, even with all the riches and latest technology on it, if it has a poor foundation, it could crumble when a calamity strikes. In the same way, that is how vulnerable an individual, a marriage, a family, a team, a community, and even a society can be without a solid foundation. That is why there are people who appear to be doing well, and then for whatever reason become involved with drugs, divorce, suicide, and violent crimes. Building a solid foundation starts from the base (back to basics). For *an individual* this means meeting his basic needs first in all six areas: spiritual, mental, emotional, physical, social, and financial. For if there are six foundations and one or two are neglected, the house will still crumble.

A *community* or a *society* cannot be expected to be well if its *individuals* are not well. Building a solid foundation does not work backward like building from the roof down. If we wish to have a healthy and solid community and society, then we need to make the effort to care and provide for each individual's needs first. Once that is taken care of, then the following can be expected:

more stable SOCIETY
⇧
more stable COMMUNITIES
⇧
stronger TEAMS/GROUPS
⇧
stronger, stable FAMILIES
⇧
more stable, lasting MARRIAGE/RELATIONSHIPS
⇧
a secure, stable INDIVIDUALS

In the process of our self-discovery as individuals and as a society, we are to remember *our children*. Our beloved children are everywhere—at home, school, church, movie theaters, game stores, on the Internet, etc. Children learn from their parents, teachers, church leaders, government and community leaders, business owners, movie industry leaders, sports players, movie and TV stars, and all the other adults who are their supposedly *role models*. Our children offer no excuses for our pure irresponsibility and misdoing (that is why rebellion of all forms comes). They are, however, very smart and forgiving to understand and accept

Now, What's Next?

that we adults are not perfect, provided they can see that we are sincerely doing our best. Instead of the home, school and government going back and forth on who has more responsibility in teaching our children basic conduct, remember that it takes a village, an entire community, to raise these children. If we don't get our acts together, if we do not learn that we need teamwork, working together to achieve better results, then we soon-to-be seniors will just have to watch and feel the consequences.

As we continue to share our dreams and visions, let us find a way to build those strong foundations together. Be a brother, a sister, a neighbor, a friend. Let us also be a partner to each other. Let us be actively involved with our schools, churches, and communities, even in governing bodies. We can learn to be team players again—the team of people who care, the real *winning team*!

> *"There is enough in the world for everyone to have plenty to live on happily and to be at peace with his neighbors."*
>
> – Harry S. Truman

Let us bring HOPE to our communities…

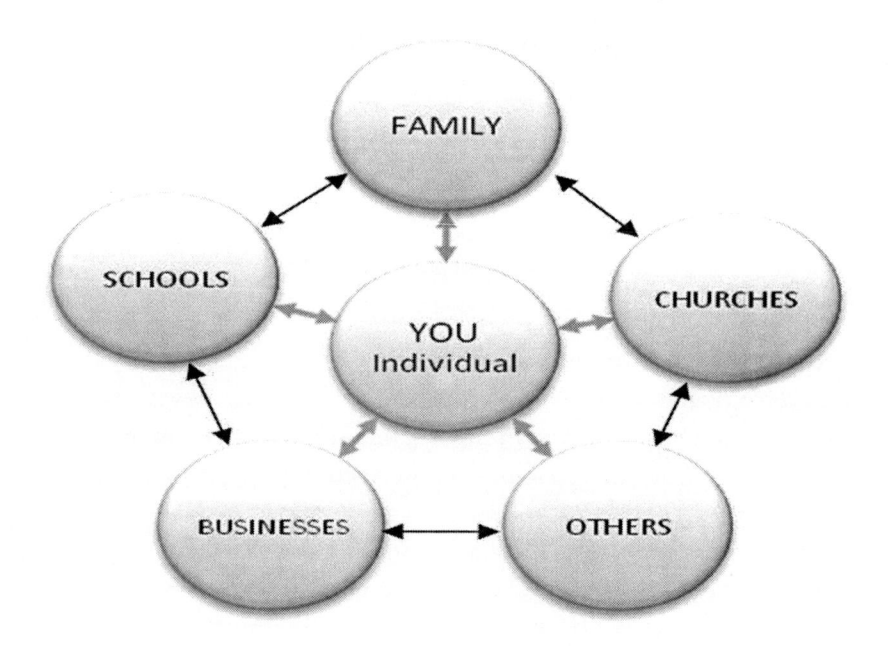

Be a PARTNER!

If we can only bring individuals, families, schools, churches, businesses, and other segments of our community together, it will make a world of difference for all of us.

> *"Somewhere out there is a unique place for you to help others – a unique role for you to fill that only you can fill."*
> Thomas Kinkade, American artist

> *"Until he extends the circle of his compassion to all living things, man will not himself find peace."*
> Albert Schweitzer, Alsatian theologian, philosopher, physician, and musician

What can be done?

1. More *public awareness* and open discussion of issues, problems, and situations that affect us as individuals, families, societies, and as a nation.

2. Provide more *health and total wellness education* and *financial literacy* for all age groups.

3. *Encourage* more *expression of dreams, talents,* and *creativities* among our children at home, at school, everywhere. Establish more schools and centers that allow plenty of space for children to explore to develop their God-given talents, personal development, and character building, to develop social skills to get along well with others, as well as business and leadership orientation—so we don't only prepare our children for future careers but for better life in the future.

4. Create more *comprehensive* and *integrated community resource centers* that people can call or go to in their communities for information, education, and training, for resources of various needs and support system addressing, not just one problem but total wellness and financial security.

5. More *senior retirement communities* with plenty of space, activities, care, and opportunities to volunteer and be involved or contribute to our youth and community wellness.

6. Establish *transition homes and projects* for the veterans who have served our country and homeless people who may have lost their jobs or other circumstances, especially families with children who just need a break and can use temporary support, encouragement, job skills, or small business training and counseling to be able to successfully get back on their feet again. Creating simple-to-implement *micro-loan programs* could benefit many.

7. Build more *rehabilitation* and *restoration communities* instead of more jails for minors or first-time offenders, especially for the youth, equipped with education, training, and counseling programs that help individuals be more prepared to go back to society and their families.

Life calls us to TAKE ACTION—positive, meaningful and productive action. Meaningful life comes from knowing that we are giving our best to live harmoniously with our Creator, with others, and with ourselves. *Loving God with all our being, and loving others as we love ourselves* are the only two things we need to remember, and the rest of the good things for each of us will follow.

It is time for us, for our land, for our county to heal and be well again. When we align with God and His principles, work harmoniously with His plan for each of us and the environment we are in, we cannot go wrong. The energy forces within us and around us will bring that desire into reality. *"Come what may, the best of life is still to come!"*

> *"I expect to pass through life but once. If, therefore, there be any kindness I can show, or any good thing I can do to any fellow being, let me do it now, for I shall not pass this way again."*
>
> William Penn, founder
> of Pennsylvania, USA

Yes! The Secrets Work!

God bless YOU! God bless AMERICA and EVERYONE and every NATION around the world whom God loves so much!

A Final Note from the Author

This is truly not the end but just the beginning…a fresh, new beginning. As I close this book, there are three challenges or questions that I want to share. These are now my personal goals and dreams:
1. *Is it really possible to be totally debt free, to owe nothing but love?*
2. *Could it be possible that more people (more than just the one to three percent) can live in real dignity of mankind, earn and live with more than just enough to survive each day, and have a happy, healthy, and fulfilled life called "abundance"?*
3. *Could it be possible that within three months, at least 3 million books will be sold, so that at least 3 million people can benefit, including those who will read, believe, and take action to fulfill their dreams and meet their potential; help feed the hungry children of the world; bring more human dignity and opportunity to this world's poorest of the poor by providing them better shelters and self-sustaining communities; assist in health and medical missions for total wellness programs; support local projects that bring financial literary and the best quality of life for individuals in their communities? The 333 HOPE Challenge (Health and Opportunity for People Everywhere)*

I am smiling, as I believe that nothing is impossible to those who believe and take action. I truly believe the fulfillment of these visions and heart desires will just be a matter of time. Will you be a part of fulfilling these visions? Will you be one of the first 3 Million Mountain Movers who will do the seemingly impossible?

How about you? What are your dreams, goals, heart desires? Are they written? Put them in writing and focus each day on fulfilling what you wrote. It will be just a matter of time as you persist to believe, never giving up, knowing and trusting God that He already intended those good gifts

Now, What's Next?

for you...and so the universe, under God's direction and your continuous belief, will make these dreams come to pass!

I am rallying for you. Shall we keep in touch and share our wonderful blessings and dream fulfillments? Will you please share these marvelous secrets or discoveries to others also,-and encourage them to do the same so we can reach as many people as possible as soon as possible? We all need to help or support one another to create a better world in which to live and to pass on to our children and grandchildren. Thank you very much for being a part of these shared dreams, visions, and missions!

May this moment and time be your best time ever!

Sincerely,
Anolia Orfrecio Facun

Individuals, Groups, and Organizations Making a Difference

There are well-known *organizations* like *American Red Cross, Salvation Army, United Way*, various *churches, and organizations* that we encourage people to be involved with or contribute to by volunteering or other means. Here are few less noticed individuals and-organizations who have, against all odds, created amazing stories and are our unsung heroes. Aware or not, they are making a huge difference in our society and in our world. We salute you!

Dennis – I don't even have his full name, but I will always remember him and would like to acknowledge him because he made an impact on me and so many who watched him marvelously sing on the stage of one of the cruises we've been on. Dennis is so talented, happy, and full of life (just having a blast and expressing that he still has many dreams and tasks to do). Today and every day, he will be a great inspiration to many. He moved me to finally finish this book, inspired me it could be done, that I no longer had any excuse. Dennis is blind with some physical so-called deformities and needed to be assisted to go to the stage. Each of us CAN.

Mom from Florida – A very moving story of a parent who was faced with the most difficult decision she had to make in her entire life, a decision that was against everyone's advice. She took all the chances. Against all odds, oppositions, and continuous challenges, hers is one of the most inspiring stories, which is creating a huge impact in the lives of many who will hear and be tremendously blessed by the model childcare center they established in Florida. The center she and her family established should be a model for the entire country. (I have not reached her yet to ask permission to put her name or their center in this book).

Terri Khonsari – Author of the book *Raising a Superstar*, Khonsari's is the inspiring story of a single mom who raised her daughter alone in spite of poverty and all types of hardship in life. She raised a brilliant, talented, super-achiever child and at the same time was a caring, model citizen who was going places in the world to spread goodwill. It's an amazing story, and in her book she shares simple strategies on how to bring out the brilliance in every child. To parents and teachers, this is a book worth checking out.

All three great people above I would not have met if I had not make the decision to attend the *Bob Proctor cruise*, which I am so grateful for. It was meant for a purpose, as it made an impact for the rest of my life and for sure impacted the many who attended that cruise seminar. See, it only takes a spark.

Clemente –He is a personal hero in my life. He was from another country seeking to live a better life in America. One day I noticed how hard he worked on our garden. Having a conversation with him, I was concerned. I wondered, how do they live, seven people in a one-bedroom apartment? How will they continue to survive as he gets older and God forbid gets sick, and will he be able to retire at all? I can't leave those thoughts, so I tried to help him. It wasn't easy; it took almost two years. Now he owns a very successful landscaping business with his brothers, earning six figures income, and his family is living a good life in a three bedroom, two bath home, which he owns, settled in an almost half-acre lot. Clemente came to America without any formal education, couldn't speak English, and had no credit history. He had to find means to teach himself how to read, write, and speak in English, and do the business…and he did.

There are many more amazing stories that I have seen and heard. There is this paraplegic man who did water skiing, parasailing, etc., Joni, who wrote a book with her teeth, and more. Instead of thinking of the problems and cares of these worlds, I focus on these real people who are true inspirations, for they, too, have adversities, but they have declared their victories instead.

Doctors without borders – I salute this independent medical team of doctors around the globe who have dedicated their lives out there in places that needed the most help for those who would not otherwise be reached with care and medical attention. They are living miracles to humanity. Their Nobel Prize is well-deserved, and we hope more will follow their examples. *www.doctorswithoutborders.org*

Habitat for Humanity – This non-profit organization started in 1976 and has built and rehabilitated more than three hundred thousand homes in partnership with those who otherwise cannot afford to have their homes. Its mission is seeking to eliminate poverty housing and homelessness. With its worldwide affiliates, they continue to invite people of all backgrounds to help build simple, decent affordable houses together in partnership with people in need. *www.habitat.org*

ANCOP USA/Gawad Kalinga– Gawad Kalinga, meaning "to care," brings to the poorest of the poor (the homeless squatters living on shanties most of the time on garbage dumps, which seems impossible) their own homes in beautiful, colorful, thriving communities. This volunteer group started in the Philippines, then the world noticed and now has hundreds of thousands of volunteers around the globe who are becoming aware that poverty and homelessness, not only in physical terms but in the spirit of dignity of humankind, can be reversed or slowly but surely can dramatically be decreased or eliminated through faith, team effort, and genuine Christian stewardship and care for mankind. *www.ancopusa.org* / *www.gawadkalinga.org*

The Special Olympics – A marvelous idea to highlight the tremendous talents and abilities that our younger generation has in spite of some mental or physical limitations. Yet they are successfully able to share with us the joy of watching the reality that "anyone can do it," that "nothing is impossible to those who desire to achieve their dreams." *www.specialolympics.org*

Big Brothers and Sisters – Millions of children in our nation and around the globe need to know that someone cares and can use an adult figure to give them encouragement and hope, men and women of all ages who are willing to share some of their time and knowledge to help nurture these young children who desperately need a buddy who cares, a role model in their lives. More volunteers are needed. *www.bbbsa.org*

Make A Difference Day – This is a national volunteering day being celebrated every fourth Saturday of October since 2000 and has inspired millions of individuals and groups to do something good for a day, creating an impact in the lives of the recipients, the volunteers, and their communities. Plan to join next time on one of the projects in your area or help initiate a much needed one in your community. Every effort counts. *www.makeadifferenceday.com*

Local Food Pantries/Second Harvest – More than ever much needed support in our local areas, in every community, will be greatly appreciated. Join the great men and women who have sacrificed and dedicated a great portion of their lives to volunteer to help others. Participate in food drives, collect clothes, beddings and other winter needs. Be sensitive of those you are in touch with who may need help. If you will ever need help, do not hesitate to receive. That's what this effort is all about, teamwork, all of us working together, supporting one another. *www.secondharvest.org* Similar organizations are: *Feed the Children* and *Feed333.org*

Spend your time and energy wisely! Be productive. Do not just read the bad news or fiction pocketbooks. Instead read and hear inspirational stories, read valuable how-to books. It is healthy for you and your environment. Then you can participate in making a difference to a person, a family, or your community.

There are a lot more individuals, medical missions, churches, non-profit organizations, and even business groups out there, local and international, that I was not able to mention in this book, but I still want to recognize and express my deep appreciation. My salutation to all of you and a huge "THANK YOU" for *making a difference!*

Book of Life Reference List

The Book of Life contains living words that can set you *free* and help you live an abundant and victorious life. These living words have remained true and meaningful to me all my life. No matter what happens, they have been my faithful guiding light.

And you shall know the truth, and the truth shall make you free.
John 8:32

The thief (enemy) does not come except to steal, and to kill, and to destroy. I have come that they may have life, and that they may have it more abundantly.
John 10:10

For God so loved the world that He gave His only begotten Son, that whoever believes in Him should not perish but have everlasting life.
John 3:16

Jesus said to him, *"I am the way, the truth, and the life. No one comes to the Father except through Me."*
John 14:6

For you did not receive the spirit of bondage again to fear, but you received the Spirit of adoption by whom we cry out, "Abba, Father." The Spirit Himself bears witness with our spirit that we are children of God.
Romans 8:16

Jesus said to him, *"You shall love the Lord your God with all your heart, with all your soul, and with all your mind."* This is the first and great commandment. And the second is like it: *"You shall love your neighbor as yourself."*
Matthew 22:37

And we know that all things work together for good to those who love God, to those who are the called according to His purpose.
>Romans 8:28

For we do not wrestle against flesh and blood, but against principalities, against powers, against the rulers of the darkness…"
>Ephesians 6:12

Yet in all these things we are more than conquerors through Him who loved us
>Romans 8:37

Fear not, for I am with you; do not be dismayed, for I am your God. I will strengthen you, Yes, I will help you, I will uphold you with My righteous right hand.
>Isaiah 41:10

…if you have faith as a mustard seed, you will say to this mountain, "Move from here to there," and it will move; and nothing will be impossible for you.
>Matthew 17:20

But seek first the kingdom of God and His righteousness, and all these things shall be added to you.
>Matthew 6:33

Believe! Be a mountain mover!

Declaration

This could be one of the most important steps that you will take in your life. If the *words* you say and *believe with all your heart and mind* determine the results that can affect your life, then *so be it*. Today you can make *a personal declaration*.

A *declaration* is a formal statement or proclamation just like what the government, judicial, or church officials do, like the *Declaration of Independence*. Today you can reclaim your best life intended for you by making a declaration to yourself and to the world. Below is a sample.

You can do this best by going back to your mirror. It may be uncomfortable or seem silly at first, but as you take your life more seriously and have a great anticipation of what is about to come to you, you will find this declaration a very meaningful event in your life. Read first, repeat the process until you internalize the words, and eventually the words will come out naturally with your full belief and passion. That is when you are ready. *Are you ready?*

I declare that...

I have the truth, and therefore I am now FREE!

I am more than special, marvelously created and unique.

I am no longer allowing this world's thief to steal my joy and peace, nor to destroy my relationships and good future. I declare to receive the abundant life that is intended for me.

I accept that God loves me, believe and accept His Son as my Lord and Savior and the everlasting life He promised.

I am no longer in bondage of fear. Instead I will live in the bond of God's love, my Abba Father, for me. I know that all things will work together for good for me. I will live with purpose, and my life will be lived to the fullest.

I am more than a conqueror through Him who loves me!

I am victorious, and I am ready to move mountains!

Signed: _____ Date: _____

DO IT ANYWAY!

People are often unreasonable, illogical, and self-centered;

Forgive them anyway.

If you are kind, people may accuse you of selfish, ulterior motives;

Be kind anyway.

If you are successful, you will win some false friends and some true enemies;

Be successful anyway.

If you are honest and frank, people may cheat you;

Be honest and frank anyway.

What you spend years building, someone could destroy overnight;

Build anyway.

If you find serenity and happiness, they may be jealous;

Be happy anyway.

The good you do today, people will often forget tomorrow;

Do good anyway.

Give the world the best you have, and it may never be enough;

Give the world the best you've got anyway.

You see, in the final analysis, it is between you and God;

It was never between you and them anyway.

by Mother Teresa

About the Author

Anolia Orfrecio Facun, or *"Leah,"* came to the United States of America from Philippines at age twenty two with a suitcase and a few dollars in hand, knowing nobody nor have a home to go to. She had a dream to be a nurse forever. She first lived in Miami, Florida, for ten years then moved to California where she resides now with her family.

Throughout her life in the USA, she held three licenses: a registered nurse license for fifteen years, experiencing many areas and responsibilities in the nursing, medical, and teaching field; an insurance license, dealing with insurance and other financial services for about seven years; and a real estate license for four years to have more exposure and further specialize on RE investments. With her passion for teaching and preventive health approach, she considered her later two careers as her version of preventive medicine and community health nursing, as other means of helping people while helping self. She has received, together with her husband as life and business partner, numerous awards and recognitions from her business and community involvements.

Anolia and her husband, Victor, have traveled extensively to many beautiful places in the US and the world. They have three beautiful grown children who joined some of their trips. She feels blessed for being able to live a very colorful, meaningful, and purposeful life. Now she wants to share with others, who otherwise may not have a chance, her gathered knowledge and gained experiences of over twenty-five years so that they may benefit also.

With her hectic business and travel schedule, she always find the time to follow her passion of teaching and helping people through public awareness seminars and active involvement with schools, churches, and community projects and programs. You may contact her by going to her website: www.YesTheSecretsWork.com

She acknowledges God to be her ultimate source for everything.

Free Bonus Gifts!!!

Thank you for purchasing Yes! The Secrets Work! Welcome to the exciting world of new discovery as you unlock your true potential and purpose in life. As a special bonus, we're giving you two gifts:

Bonus Gift #1: Life's ABC's

Gain new meaning to our alphabet and everyday word use.

Bonus Gift #2: 37 Ways to Make a Difference to Yourself & Others

Making a difference is not just a scheduled event or activity, but a moment any time when a person finds it in his/her heart to do something good, to care or to share, or to make a voluntary contribution to another individual, a community or our society. Here's how you can begin.

Ready to get your free gifts?
Visit our site at:

http://www.yesthesecretswork.com/bonusgift.html

Explore our website and take advantage of the many helpful resources we have available. When you register to our site you will continue to access or receive YTSW's valuable information, resources, and updates on our upcoming projects and events.

Together, We Can Make a World of Difference!

Thank you and best wishes,
Leah Facun & the YTSW Team

Emergency Contact Numbers And Other Resources:

Note: Phone numbers and websites may change anytime. Consult your directories or call information when needed.

9-1-1 – Fire, police, and paramedics (life-threatening situations).

2-1-1 – Any other non-emergency resources and support line, by *United Way*. When you do not know who to call, this connects you with hundreds of community services, twenty-four hours a day, including info and referrals for basic needs, child and elder care, counseling, employment, health, immigration assistance, volunteering, etc.

www.ready.gov – Earthquake, emergency, and disaster preparedness information.

1-800-569-4287 - US Dept. HUD (Housing Urban Development) national toll free number for list of HUD approved housing counseling agencies.

1-888-995-HOPE (4673) – Homeownership Preservation Foundation can helpwhen facing Foreclosure, HUD certified. Or visit www.995hope.org.

1-866-557-2227 – NFCC/Homeowner Crisis Resource Center available in your area. Or visit www.housinghelpnow.org.

1-800-388-2227 – National Foundation for Credit Counseling. Or visit www.debtadvice.org. Providing debt management plans.

1-877-712-1452 – Consumer Credit Counseling.

1-800-222-1222 – Twenty-four hour Poison Control Center (call 911 for emergencies)

1-800-342-2437 – Communicable Disease Control & Prevention

1-800-222-3463 – Missing Children Hotline

1-800-344-6000 – Child Abuse Hotline (Children Services Bureau)

1-800-799-7233 – National Domestic Violence Hotline

1-800-479-3339 – Suicide and Crisis Intervention (twenty-four hour)

1-800-772-1213 – Social Security Office

1-800-500-6411 – Women, Infants, and Children (WIC Program)

1-800-638-2772 – US Consumer Product Safety Commission Hotline

1-800-669-4000 – US Equal Employment Opportunity Commission

1-800-448-3543 – American Red Cross Blood Services

When you or someone you know needs help, do not hesitate. There is help available. Avoid scams. Contact the mentioned resources first. Ask for referrals when necessary. Also check your local phone book for *Local Food Pantries/Second Harvest* for immediate temporary help. It also contains *First Aid & Survival Guides* and many other emergency and helpful service numbers that you can call. Please advise us of other resources and groups or services that you find recommendable so we may add on our list.

For comments, request for group presentations or fundraising partnership, you may contact us by visiting our website:

www.YesTheSecretsWork.com

BUY A SHARE OF THE FUTURE IN YOUR COMMUNITY

These certificates make great holiday, graduation and birthday gifts that can be personalized with the recipient's name. The cost of one S.H.A.R.E. or one square foot is $54.17. The personalized certificate is suitable for framing and will state the number of shares purchased and the amount of each share, as well as the recipient's name. The home that you participate in "building" will last for many years and will continue to grow in value.

Here is a sample SHARE certificate:

Sample certificate shown:
HABITAT FOR HUMANITY
THIS CERTIFIES THAT
YOUR NAME HERE
HAS INVESTED IN A HOME FOR A DESERVING FAMILY
1985-2005
TWENTY YEARS OF BUILDING FUTURES IN OUR COMMUNITY ONE HOME AT A TIME
1200 SQUARE FOOT HOUSE @ $65,000 = $54.17 PER SQUARE FOOT
This certificate represents a tax deductible donation. It has no cash value.

YES, I WOULD LIKE TO HELP!

I support the work that Habitat for Humanity does and I want to be part of the excitement! As a donor, I will receive periodic updates on your construction activities but, more importantly, I know my gift will help a family in our community realize the dream of homeownership. **I would like to SHARE in your efforts against substandard housing in my community!** *(Please print below)*

PLEASE SEND ME _____ SHARES at $54.17 EACH = $ $_____

In Honor Of: _____

Occasion: (Circle One)   HOLIDAY   BIRTHDAY   ANNIVERSARY
           OTHER: _____

Address of Recipient: _____

Gift From: _____ *Donor Address:* _____

Donor Email: _____

I AM ENCLOSING A CHECK FOR $ $_____ PAYABLE TO HABITAT FOR HUMANITY <u>OR</u> PLEASE CHARGE MY VISA OR MASTERCARD *(CIRCLE ONE)*

Card Number _____ Expiration Date: _____

Name as it appears on Credit Card _____ Charge Amount $ _____

Signature _____

Billing Address _____

Telephone # Day _____ Eve _____

PLEASE NOTE: Your contribution is tax-deductible to the fullest extent allowed by law.
Habitat for Humanity • P.O. Box 1443 • Newport News, VA 23601 • 757-596-5553
www.HelpHabitatforHumanity.org